MW01656960

12 Faces Of Sober

A Veteran's Battle with Alcoholism &

Kicking the Deadly Addiction

KENNETH L. WATSON JR.

Copyright © 2020
All rights reserved.
No part of this publication may be
reproduced or transmitted in any form or by any means,
electronic, or mechanical, including photocopying,
recording, or by any information storage and retrieval
system, without permission in writing from the publisher.
Published by Kenneth L. Watson Jr.
7055 Blanding Blvd
Unit 441473
Jacksonville, FL 32222
United States
Cover Design by Manny Brizuela
Web Design by Marcel Oliver
Editor Patricia Ogilvie

1st Edition

ISBN: 9798671486933

DEDICATION

To the circle of people who have helped and supported me on my journey through sobriety.

Table of Contents

ACKNOWLEDGMENTS

Thank- you readers. Thank-you brothers, sisters, and friends who believed in me. This is for you, for your courage and dedication to helping me make my life better. And now, I want to help you make your life even better.

CHAPTER 1—INTRODUCTION TO OPEN FACE

This book, *12 Faces of Sober* is my journey in which I, Kenneth Lee Watson, Jr. *Lived it, Seen it, and Done it* when it came to alcohol. The title derives from the twelve years of my alcoholism versus the twelve months and beyond being sober, and some of the faces I made during those chaotic and joyful times. For 12 years alcohol was my best friend and it controlled my life. This story will give you a better understanding of what my life was like before I started drinking, then to go on and struggle with a powerful addiction to a poisonous chemical. I believe alcoholism is hereditary, but by the same token, can be the exact opposite—life not drinking or life being a social drinker.

I would like to make a disclaimer: Some names have been changed to protect the privacy of the individuals mentioned. I don't need anyone making a profit from being discussed in MY book! Ok, now that I have that out of the way, let's get started on why this book may help you. Some come from a bloodline of alcoholics, work with alcoholics, and have seen friends and family members who suffer from the disease. I have realized that I am allergic to alcohol. My body doesn't react like others.

This book is for those who drink and those like myself who don't drink, but struggled with alcoholism. This is for that service member deployed going through withdrawals because they aren't allowed to drink, and for the family and friends who witnessed someone struggle with addiction.

My journey starts with where I grew up, my teenage years and college years. Leaving California at twenty and relocating to Minnesota and the life that I lived there pretty much for five years. My move to Arizona, where my life changed in terms of relationships and the increase in alcohol. Touch on in-depth, different relationship issues and how alcohol was around me, and how it led to pretty much my tolerance increasing. In terms of what I drank, do I want to embrace this different lifestyle or different culture in terms of what I was used to in Minnesota—being a social drinker and then going to Arizona and just pretty much turning it into a full-fledged alcoholic.

I was dealing with relationships that I would say were more serious in Arizona than dating in other cities. Phoenix is when I started to abuse alcohol and dealt with physical and verbal altercations. My first engagement, how that all came together, how it pretty much ended, and the strife that disconnected us, was dealing with an abortion and more. My arrest due to that relationship pretty much changed my life. How it was like if I didn't get up out of Arizona, I probably would have ended up going back to jail on a longer stay than just for the night.

The embarrassment of bouncing from house to house when I moved back to Minnesota: from my mom's house, my nephew's house, my dad's house, back to my mom's house, back to my dad's house. I was going through some real true pain because I was dealing with an abortion. I was already drinking, but I probably increased it by ten. I mean by that, it was just ten more things that I would drink if, that's daily consumption that I would probably in Minnesota, and it only increased, increased, and increased.

Each time I was in treatment, I would always make a plan to do something, and that goal would seem to get accomplished. When I was in treatment (first time), the counsellor asked me, "What are you going to do when you get out?" I said, I'm going to join the Army. His response, "Why? It's not going to benefit you." I finished the conversation with, "what do I have to lose?" Everything he was saying went in one ear and out the other. This was the day I was discharged.

While in the Army, I was also engaged a second time. I'll discuss that relationship, the good and the bad and how we remain friends still today. I've been there for her She's been there for me. She's cool with my family, so don't get anything twisted. 2004 is when we met. So, we've been friends. We tried the relationship thing and it didn't work, but at least we are still friends. The struggles I faced in the military after that relationship didn't work out.

When I got out of my first engagement, my ex-wife was right there calling. It was almost like this was a plot, or I was a target, and she was going to get me regardless. I'll discuss that marriage, the ins and outs, the good and the bad within that—the treatment that I received from her family and then so on. But like I said, that's why I'm kind of distant now in terms of like relationship with people's parents. But, then, of course, you want to protect your child or family member, but by the same token, you got to focus on who is truly in the wrong. I was accused of infidelity and everything, but there's no proof, no evidence that there was infidelity. I was dealing with three disrespectful kids, the involvement of a baby daddy who's currently a drug dealer. My issues with him and how a bogus CPS report was filed. My bold prediction in August 2015 that the marriage would not last much longer after getting out of the Army.

She physically assaulted me, got arrested. And I want to

touch on this, in the introduction, because this is just juicy enough. Technically she cannot work for the state of Arizona, or maybe it might be revoked for the whole country, but I don't think she can practice nursing. She can be in a supervisory type role, but because of that record, she has a misdemeanor, and it's going to sit on her record for the rest of her life unless she gets it expunged. But I'm sure getting the government to expunge it is very difficult.

Stints in rehab: The first one was in Minneapolis, Minnesota in 2008. The second one was in Alexandria, Virginia 2014. The third one was in Phoenix, Arizona 2016. Finally, my last and most meaningful stint in rehab was in St. Cloud, Minnesota 2016.

My experience traveling sober: New York, New Jersey, South Africa, Washington, D.C., Ohio, North Carolina, California, Mississippi, and Florida, where I reside in my birth city of Jacksonville. This is compared to not traveling while married because she was so jealous. Phoenix was the only destination somebody wanted to go to all the time.

I have a big support network consisting of childhood friends in San Diego, California, friends from college in St Cloud, Minnesota, Atlanta Georgia, folks in Phoenix, Arizona, my Army family in Fort Bragg, Fort Lee, Fort Bliss, and Fort Jackson, and other people that I have met along the way. I would like to say a big THANK-YOU for never judging or given up on me.

I would also like to give a special thanks and appreciation to the following individuals:

Whitney (My SWEETS), I appreciate you because you've pushed me more than any other woman that I've dealt with. And that says a lot and I appreciate you putting up with me 'cause sometimes it's hard and difficult, but just know that I love you with all my heart and 2020 is going to be our year and beyond because, "teamwork makes the dream work." Well, we're on our way. Meeting you in October 2018 until the present day has pretty much changed my life dramatically. I almost quit grad school right at the end of my program before I met you because I just felt like I couldn't type, I couldn't write, and couldn't do research.

As of right now, I have chosen not to work. I started the PhD program, but had to drop out due to some personal circumstances. But that doesn't mean that I can't go back. That is the plan eventually, once I get settled here in Jacksonville and try to really get a routine ‘cause doing the PhD is a real commitment, and now it's been a lot of conflicts with time and scheduling. I still intend on getting a PhD, it's just a matter of time, maybe 2021. By then, I should be good to go with everything. I think that the book is a start because I do plan on eventually doing speaking engagements. Everything is going to fall together. The stuff that I went through the anger, the frustration, the destroying of property, getting into some really heated arguments, getting arrested, being homeless, having so many run-ins with the police in different states, and being in handcuffs in the military.

My mom, Earnestine, has always wanted the best for me. She never really liked the idea of me drinking because I reminded her so much of my dad when I was drunk. Was my protector when those racist teachers said I would amount to having nothing more than an associate degree. Stressed the level of importance when it came to education. She deserves the highest degree that I have because if it weren’t for her, I wouldn't have applied to graduate school. She said, “just try it out and see what happens”. So, Mom, I love you. I know that I've made a lot of mistakes growing up as a child, as an adult, but just know that I'm happy that you're still alive to see the changes that I have made in my life and the fact that we talk every day at ten o'clock in the morning and I sometimes notice that I get busy and I forget what time it is, but I appreciate you.

My Pops: we haven’t had the best relationship. I think that you wanted to live a life as “Papa Was a Rolling

Stone," but not necessarily with being married and having kids, but just more or less like you wanted to run wild and run free. Still, you got married, so you continue to run wild and run free, but you just don't know the impact that you had on the family, your step kids, or your kids. But I appreciate you because I've learned a lot from you. I've been able to cut corners in life that you couldn't do. You had to work forty plus years to my ten to fifteen years. The only thing I need you for the rest of my life is to be my father.

My oldest brother Michael, I appreciate all the prayers over the years. We are eleven years apart, and by the time I was ten, you were overseas serving in the Air Force. So a lot of years, you weren't around as much as I wished to get brotherly advice. But once I became an adult, it was and still is great to have some in-depth conversations about current events. I can't wait to take some of those international trips with you—much love and respect.

My brother Anthony, You have been more like a father to me then a big brother. We're ten years apart. You taught me the game. I'm sorry, he taught me the game. I just realized, you know, I remember we went to the buffet, it was me, you, Felton and Derek and you guys just hit me with the whole intervention, and I was so fucking mad, and I had been drinking that morning too, but I took it to heart, but it was just not my time to take that advice.

My sister Laquisha, She's been like a second mom and thru the years held me accountable for my mistakes and gave me some of the best advice and support. I appreciate the fact that I've been able to call you over the years about my issues with the women I dated. Thank-You for being one of my biggest cheerleaders during my sober journey. I love and appreciate you for that.

My sister Lakeia, I don't know how to explain it, but I'm just going to say that I love you, and hopefully we can get our shit together so that we can be better as far as a relationship. It doesn't matter how long it takes, but I love you. It'll get fixed.

Mike, my oldest nephew, I've tried my best to kick the same game that Anthony kicked to me, especially when you were younger. I've appreciated every conversation that we've had, good or bad. One day we will be business owners. I appreciate the fact that you let me stay with you guys when I first came back. No money will ever cover what you've done for me, but I love you, and I respect you as a man, and I'm proud of you as you know, for who you are. You're a wise person. Just use your smarts because you got fucking ridiculous amounts of it.

Marcel, I'm proud of you and what you have accomplished. Keep working hard in school. Change is good. So be prepared for anything thrown in your direction. Make the decision that best suits Marcel. Skies the limit to what you can do and accomplish moving forward in life.

Janelle, you're almost grown. You only have one year left, and you will be off to college. We are going to butt heads, and we're not going to always agree, but just guarantee that I got much love for you. You are smart and can do whatever you put your mind too.

Quentin, as the next dual-sport athlete. You might want to say tri-sport athlete. I want to see you play all three sports; baseball, basketball and football. You might want to throw in soccer, but I guarantee you're going to the pros. But the only thing is you have to really control your attitude on the court. The refs will respect you. Refs will start making those calls that they once missed. So, sportsmanship is the best thing. EDUCATION is what will carry you further in society once sports are over.

My brother-in-law Don Oliver, aka Off Da Heezy Fa Sheezy. I appreciate what you do for the family. Thank-you for showing me how to change the oil in a car and how to change a tire. We have some memories worthy of a movie. I meant what I said about you being one of my best friends: from taking me fishing to attending all my graduations. Thanks for being a real ass person. I look forward to making more memories. Hopefully, you guys come to Florida soon to see how I'm living. Love you, Bro!

Make sure to follow *#12FacesofSober* on YouTube, search klw3434@gmail.com or you can also search me by Kenneth L. Watson, Jr. on all media platforms. Needless to say, this book is from my heart. This book is my pride and joy. If I left stuff out, it could be because I just don't want to talk about it. I don't want anybody to come after me. But if they do, as I said, they can write their own book. This is the story of my life, and it's definitely 100% accurate because I don't have time to make stuff up. This is me. This is who I am. This is what I stand for. I admit, yes, I am an alcoholic, and I'm going to die an alcoholic. It took me to get the fuck out of Arizona to understand there's still more life to live. You can do this; you can survive; you can be independent. Stuff that I couldn't do when I was in my twenties or my thirties.

CHAPTER 2—EARLY YEARS OF DRINKING: CURIOUS FACE

I was born in Jacksonville, Florida, on August 2, 1979. I'm the youngest of five kids: two brothers, two sisters. Pops was in the Navy and we moved around. I am not going to say quite a bit, but we went from Jacksonville, Florida to New London, Connecticut, from 1979 to 1982. In 1982 we moved to San Diego, California, where most of my memories growing up came from that city. Why does this tie into *12 Faces of Sober*?

On Friday nights, Pops would usually get drunk or go to a bar or club doing God knows what. And when he came home, he tended to blast records, and I didn't understand it. I couldn't figure out like why. you know, it was like, he had two lives. It was like the guy who got up to go to work Monday through Friday and then Friday, Saturday, and Sunday, it was a guy who got drunk—and not really knowing that eventually, that would be something that would be my life too. But instead of it just being Friday, Saturday, and Sunday, it was Monday through Sunday, January to December, and all points in between. My love for music stemmed from my alcoholic father. In a lot of ways at that time, I didn't understand it. You know, when you're that age, they don't really give you the definition of everything. I didn't really understand it, but it seemed like that was the norm. So, I guess I was used to it.

So, it was kind of like, you know, I got to play, go to school Monday through Friday, preschool, day-care, whatever you want to call it, kindergarten, first grade. And then when it came to weekends my father got drunk. where it was like, all right, Dad's going to get drunk, but will it be early, will it be late. Will he call and cuss out my uncle in Chicago, or will he just be so drunk that he would be able to get on a plane and go to Mississippi and cause a financial burden to the family? And like I said, in a lot of ways, I didn't understand it. I kind of just went with the flow, partly just like everybody else, my brothers and sisters, but maybe they got it because you know, there's a gap in age. My oldest brother's eleven years, next brother's ten years older, my sister's nine years and my other sister is like three years older than me. So, maybe they got it in a lot of ways; they understood it because, as I said, they were much older than I was at the time. But I think it was hard because I saw my father as my hero, just like any other kid growing up. An ideal person, you know, can't nobody tell you nothing bad about your father. But as time went on in a lot of ways, , I guess you can say at a young age, I grew further and further apart from my father just because of his antics. Still not knowing that in about twenty to twenty-five years later, I would be faced with some of the same problems that my father had. The only difference is that he had children and step kids, and my issues were raising other people's kids. I guess there's some type of correlation between the two.

But I think that when I really realized that it was an actual problem, I had to have been maybe like eight or nine years old. And at that time, my parents seemed to be constantly fighting, and of course, it had stuff to do with alcohol, my dad drinking and, you know, whatever. And I can recall one time just thinking like, my parents wouldn't really argue too much in front of us; they would go outside and go for a drive somewhere, but rarely ever, was it a confrontational type situation. But there was one time, and I think , at that time, I think he was either drinking Jack Daniel's or E&J or Christian Brothers. He would always drink hard liquor on top of beer. I happen to go outside, I can't remember if I was cooking or something, but I might've heard some noises or something in the back. And this particular time, I might've been like anywhere between third, fourth, or fifth grade. My mom told me to bring her a glass. That's what it was. I went outside because she asked me to bring her a glass. So, I'm sitting there thinking like, okay, you know, at the time she was a heavy Pepsi drinker. My mom doesn't, I've never seen my mom drink alcohol until that particular day. And when I took the glass out there, she grabbed my dad's bottle of alcohol, and I remember she was getting ready to pour it, and I snatched the glass because it was something that I wasn't used to seeing and I still didn't understand. And of course, my mom probably yelled at me, but I just felt that it was the right thing to do and not, you know, I didn't want to intervene in my parent's issues. But I just didn't want to see my mom drinking.

And I don't remember if she actually took that drink. But I know that we've had discussions over the years about that instance. I'm sure there were plenty more instances, but just the idea of that particular one stood out the most is what I, you know, I always repeat it and I tell the story, or my mom will bring it up to us, you know, bring it up to me.

I was twelve when I took my first drink. I drank some of my father's alcohol. And like I said, I was a kid just like anybody else, you know, my dad didn't care like I remember exactly where he would hide his alcohol. It was in the cabinet. He didn't have it out on display like some other families; they have their bottles and beverages out on display where a child can grab it. And you know, from time to time, I would just take a shot. Stuff was nasty! It was hot and burned my throat, but I'd say okay well if my dad likes it, then I don't understand why I don't like it. But at that age of ten, eleven, and twelve, I didn't understand. So, it was like, okay, this stuff could be a problem. But you know, sometimes it would go from one shot to potentially two shots, but never anything excessive, and it wasn't on a regular basis, but I just know that it was happening.

The first time I got drunk, I was in seventh grade, I think it was the summer of '92 or '91. I don't know why, it might've been close to my birthday that year. And a friend of mine was with me. I drank a lot for someone who was five-eight, five-nine, 150 pounds, and taking shots was the worst feeling. And by far, something that a twelve-year-old should not be enduring, needless to say. But I think after that time, I don't recall drinking again till I was about fourteen, and of course, I wasn't only drinking, but I started to dabble in marijuana as well., I would say like thirteen. And being that I was an athlete, you know, starting at seven, stopping at seventeen, it was like I knew when to do that and when not to. I wouldn't drink before a game, wouldn't smoke before a game. But once I got into high school, it was like, let's hurry up and play this game win or lose. Football, basketball, baseball, whatever it was. I knew by the end of the night I was going to be drunk. I was going to be high, if not both.

And I definitely wouldn't say that it was a problem in high school only because it wasn't every weekend, but it was pretty consistent, especially in the eleventh and twelfth grades. And you know, we were at a friend's house, and her parents weren't there. It was just these two teenage girls, sixteen and seventeen, that had no parental supervision, and the parents were never there, so that was the spot. We would typically go to the games, and after that we would go to their place, they were sisters. We would all chip in, pay somebody's brother or uncle or cousin or sister. And then they would just get us whatever alcohol they could get for whatever, you know, for however much money that we gave them; we would drink, and then we would go to parties and things like that. And that's where it started to kind of spiral out of control. I could say it now thinking about it because there'd be times where, like, I might drive to the party and then I'd be like, okay, yeah, yeah, let's go. And then I'd be like, no, I don't think I need to be driving his car anymore and have somebody else drive for me.

Like I said, it was never really a problem. It was just a pattern. I think that like, okay, it's Friday or Saturday, we would drink and I'm kind of like spacing it out, but it's just giving you a visual of the timeline in terms of like where I first saw the drinking, when I started drinking, and it carrying onto something heavy.

Same way in college. In college, it wasn't that big of a problem, like at least the first couple of years, you know, we would be partying in Tijuana on like a Friday or Saturday, and I definitely never drove. I would always ride with somebody, and that's how easy that it was. But I think like, I remember, at one college, like, a moment that sticks out the most; I remember when I was in Atlanta, 1999 and me and a female friend was at the Cali Picnic at the AUC, you know, universities, Morehouse, Clark, Atlanta, Morris Brown and Spellman; you know, all the organizations would get together and based upon the region, and they would party. And I don't even know how I got the alcohol. Like I said, I was nineteen. A friend of mine was from San Diego. I guess I can't remember if she was a year older than me or two years either way. You know, we went, and I guess I was just drinking everything in sight, and then somehow, I got like pretty drunk to the point where it's like I passed out, missed half of all the festivities because I was drinking. And I don't know like I said, a lot of different things, a lot of variations, you know, came into play at that time. I remember, too, because this was my first real time away from home. Like I said, I was still living in San Diego at the time, but moved to Atlanta to go to school. And it wasn't easy. And now, looking at it, I didn't understand what depression meant, but now I do.

And that was one of the issues at that time; I was depressed. You know, there was nobody there. I only knew a few people, and I wasn't as sociable as I wish I would have been. But I'm just thankful that I got that experience of the black college but not the experience of being drunk and embarrassing myself. It's like it started then, but it carried on, and it carried on throughout college. Not necessarily the junior college that I attended, which was two and two universities for my undergrad. But you know, as I said, once I got to my final, I guess you can say my last school where I got my bachelor's, wasn't necessarily a problem because, like I said, I was of age. I could have gone to the liquor store any day, every day, if I wanted to, but I didn't. because that was the life that I lived in San Diego. It was the lifestyle that I kind of lived when I was in Atlanta. The only difference was in those two cities, I was underage. And I could still get access to alcohol, and I guess you can say I drank, but it was never anything heavy. You know what I mean, like, yeah, there were a few times we would go to the bars downtown St. Cloud, and drink. Sometimes we'd walk 'cause we were crazy, and you know, in the cold and see now mind you, this was back in the early 2000s where we didn't know what the temperature was in the wintertime. It was just cold. And if we were drinking, nobody wanted to drive so we would walk. So just imagine three or four black, black, young males walking the neighborhoods of predominantly white and not being able to get into certain house parties because of the guys were intimidated by us, they thought that we were going to steal their women, which probably was the case, but at least let it happen.

But it is what it is. And I don't know, I mean at that time, I was in a situation, and you know, I think I had my own apartment. Yes, that was my first apartment. Besides the one I had in college, but that doesn’t really count because it was campus housing. But my first apartment and person I was dating, she actually I don't know. I guess she got mad. I guess she started to see that I started to drink in excess, and I had a bottle of vodka or something. We used to drink Smirnoff Vodka, hundred proof. I don't know why, but it just seemed to be the strongest to get us drunk. So, we drank it. But I know she got mad one time and tried to pour out my whole bottle. Let me tell you, I was pretty pissed off because you know, you're in my place, and you're pouring out my shit? That's the issue. But looking back at it now, I understand, and to be honest with you, probably made me want to drink more—more of like a rebellion type thing.

But after I graduated, you know, I started working in radio and it was almost like, okay, this is what they do. You know, they drink alcohol, they do drugs. But I mean, I smoked weed, but I couldn't do anything further than that. I mean, you had people that was doing coke, you had people doing ecstasy, and I'm seeing all this stuff, but by the same token, I'm still like, I am not crazy. I mean, I'm crazy, but I'm not that crazy. I would never take it any further than just marijuana or beer or alcohol. But you know, and like I said, hanging out with celebrities and they're asking for, can you get some marijuana, well, let me make some calls and I'm not going to disclose no names, but I was able to get what they needed, and it is what it is.

But I had a limit when I worked in radio. You know, like if I went to the club, it would only be two drinks. I might get two of the hardest drinks, or I might just get two Coronas. But that was my limit because I lived in Minnesota, and I wasn't really familiar with how the police were, or how they treat it. And eventually, I learned that the hard way, not no jail time, but just the idea of just getting stopped and harassed by various police departments in the Minneapolis, St. Paul, and St. Cloud areas. I understand, and that's why I just never did it. I was always scared, you know, especially because everywhere I was, it was a far drive, you know, going back home at one, two o'clock in the morning.

So, I had to be careful, and I'll give an example. This is a really, really good example to kind of get you to see my mind-set. I had met this guy when we first moved to Minnesota. playing basketball in the neighborhood. It was funny because he was like, "man, why do you spend all your money on the drinks at the club? You know, why don't you just get you a bottle, drink before you get in the club?" I was like, you know what, that makes sense. And so, this particular night, I remember too, it was a bottle of E&J and might've been like the $7.50 or something, I forgot how much, but it was definitely a lot of E&J. So, me and the dude, we were drinking in the parking lot, you know, drinking it as much as we could, as fast as we could so that we can get in the club; we could dance it off and be alright.

But my stupid ass sat there and ordered more drinks once we got in the club and the dude was like, you know, I guess he decided that he wanted to go home early. Maybe he was mad because the women weren't feeling him or whatever it was. He was ready to go, I had a buzz and wasn't sure if I could drive. And he was like, man, where are we going to do? And so, I'm like fuck it, let's drive. So, I drove and now mind you, there was a damn storm. If you've ever lived anywhere in Minnesota, those storms are no joke, especially when it's lightning. Now, like I said, I think I was only in Minnesota for maybe two to three months. So, we're driving, I forgot what, I think it was 35 E going south into downtown St. Paul. And now the roads are not like California where they got those reflective pegs on the freeway. All you got is a white line, and they're not reflective.

I'm just sitting here like, okay, it's raining super-duper hard yet I can't even freaking, fucking see. But I kept on driving. I said, man, look, just stay up, you know, stay awake. The dude kept falling asleep. Now mind you, I'm just sitting here like, okay look, man, I got to get home and safe in one piece and not get stopped by the police. Now from the club, I remember it's Club Cancun, it's white coat, white horse station or some shit, but we left the club on 35, and I'm driving, and I'm just like, man, like I'm holding onto that steering wheel for dear life. I'm paying attention to the road; the windshield wipers are barely making it clear enough for me to see what was in front.

We keep driving, you know, there's only like maybe thirteen to fifteen miles we had to go, but that drive seemed forever. We get off the freeway, I drop him off. Now at this point, I'm like, okay, I'm kind of lost because this is a new neighborhood. Like I said, I just moved there, so I wasn't really familiar with the neighborhood. I'm trying to get out of the neighborhood, back on the little main road off the freeway to get to my house or my parents' house. And in doing so, I get to the street. I see it now. Mind you, this is before GPS, like my phone might've had GPS back in the early 2000s, but I just didn't know about that function or that app or whatever.

So I get on my street, make the right turn, and another right, just driving around, and then literally I thought I was in California. But mind you, if I was on my street when I lived in California, to the right would be the 805, to the left would be houses. So, I'm driving, and I just had like a flashback as if I was there. And then I stopped, hit the brakes, put it in reverse, backed the car, and was like, holy cow! Then I went to sleep, and when I woke up the next morning, my mom was like, "what did you do?" And the car was parked backwards, crooked in the driveway. And I was like, I don't want to talk about it. And she never asked me about it again until I told her eventually in the future, but thought it was interesting, but like I knew that I couldn't drive like that anymore. So, I didn't, you know, for the five years that I lived in Minnesota. I think that was like one of the only times that I drove intoxicated. Now I've driven under the influence plenty of times, but to actually be drunk, drunk, drunk that was the first and the last in the five years I lived there.

For those five years I lived in Minnesota, I was very cautious. Because like I said, I was in a totally different state, didn't know the laws, and how strict they were. And like I said, when I got to Minnesota, I just turned twenty-one. So, it was like, I was careful. And the most important thing when I left California and got to Minnesota was like, you got to finish school. You can't delay it anymore. You wasted too much time, too much money, too much energy, too much gas to go to school, and goof-off like you were in high school. And so that's why the drinking aspect wasn't all that serious. I would make sure my classes were good Monday through Thursday. I never had classes on Fridays. And if I did, it was early in the morning before noon, and then when I go home, I would have a drink. But even then, you know, I would drink with my brother-in-law Don because my nephew Michael wasn't old enough at the time. I would go over his house, have a couple of drinks, or something like that. But then it would never be in excess because I knew I had to drive. And so that was more the importance of safety and things like that. But let me tell you, it got worse, but we'll go into that next chapter.

CHAPTER 3—LOST MY MIND IN ARIZONA

My mom and I moved to Phoenix in 2005. Relocating to a new city is never easy. I had those high hopes. I had those ambitions of wanting to work, heck work multiple jobs if I had to. But nothing really took into effect in terms of getting the job offers or even getting a phone call for a job interview; it was very difficult. Here it is, I'm coming from Minnesota where for the most part in the two years from 03–05 I stayed with a job. It wasn't the most amount of money, but it was enough to stay above water. Depression really sunk in, I didn't know anybody for one, so I ended up hanging with my brother and his friends. What came with that was a lot of drinking.

I met a few people that I dealt with as far as dating, but like I said, primarily, I dealt with two people. I dated a woman named Rossi; she was nine years older than me. Like I just mentioned, you know, I was so accustomed to hanging out with my brother and his social circle. And those people were on average nine to ten years older, if not more than that. So that's pretty much what I had to deal with and whatnot. Rossi had four kids, and I knew I shouldn't have been dealing with her on a relationship tip. It should've just been, okay; I'm going to get me some, you know, it'd be sexual and keep it moving. But because I don't know if it was so much that I was in search or yearning for a relationship, but it was more or less that I wanted to, you know, just have the title and thinking that it would be easy. And then I knew what it was like dealing with her. I knew like, this is not going to be a good situation for me, but I dealt with it anyway.

That woman was verbally abusive and wasn't afraid to get in your face and cuss you the hell out. We would go out, and in many cases, it felt like I was a babysitter. I had to watch her to make sure she didn't drink too much or take the keys away if she had been drinking. I couldn't enjoy myself if we went to functions, 'cause somebody had to be sober.

So, in a lot of ways, that's what it was. It was you know, that or it would be drama, somebody would get into it and then she wanted to jump in, and I'd be like, your too old to be doing this stuff. You know what I mean? But that's what happens when you deal with people; and deal with the women, those Southside Phoenix females as far as I'm going to call them today. But yeah, she was very abusive. I mean, I am not going to lie; she could cook her behind off, don't get it twisted, she could, but she also had her own problems, had her own issues. Needless to say, I am happy, very fortunate that that relationship didn't last, but one thing I've noticed about those types of chicks is that like they, they always lingered around for years 'cause that's kind of how it was.

We had dealt with each other for a couple of months. Everything was cool, high impact, you know, sex in spontaneous places, she introduced me to a lot of different people, and I was able to see the city, which was a good thing, but it was also a bad thing because she knew everybody. So, when a person knows everybody, that could be your problem. And that's pretty much what it was. It wasn't necessarily that I was a physical person in the relationship. Still, I did find myself being put into some very uncomfortable situations with her. I couldn't figure out and understand why; but that's what it was, and this was kind of like there in the early stages of me trying to, I guess you can say, explore alcohol a little bit more. And like I said before, you know, I drank light because I was kind of the person that was afraid of getting a DUI or anything of that nature.

Sure, enough, I mean, like I said, I never got a DUI, let alone got stopped by the police despite the numerous times that I did, you know, drove drunk. But in this relationship, like I said, and just mentioned it was a relationship that lingered and lingered, I would say off and on for about a year and a half, almost two years. But I mean, I was doing my thing, you know, I had women, but it was just something like I would go back to her, she'd go back to me, or we bumped into each other or just a random phone call. And I think that last time I'll never forget it. Like she knew I was dealing with my first fiancé and she wanted to come over and try to fuck and break up the situation.

And I was just like, you know, I asked women like, why are you hurting me? After some time, you try to come back into my life like that, which has happened numerous times. And needless to say, I was just like, holy cow. And you know, and I guess I could say, that relationship as I said, didn't last, and it was like I said, it was even awkward because this was a person that was cool or really, really good friends with my ex-wife. They were friends before they knew me, and they probably still hang with each other to this day or are acquaintances. But it just seemed to be picking up more and more. It was like I' was constantly getting drunk. And you know, I remember like scraping up pennies, nickels, and dimes to go to 7-Eleven, just to get me a $1.30 beer or get 200 pennies to get me a forty that's just how bad and how serious it was and of course my health wasn't the greatest. I was so strapped for money, I did my grocery shopping at the 99-cent store. And that's how I ate, and that's how I survived. Needless to say, I would get me about a hundred dollars' worth of groceries, and it would last the entire month. You wouldn't be able to get as much food like that if you were to go to Walmart today.

During that second stint of living in Phoenix and that second stint of living in Phoenix was three years. For the most part, those three years I was drunk. I had two serious relationships. And obviously both of them failed. But like I said, the first relationship with the older lady, I didn't really necessarily have a drinking problem. I was basically watching an alcoholic teach me how to be an alcoholic, and how to be emotional and how to be confrontational, complain about any and everything. So those are the type of things that I dealt with in that relationship. And it wasn't easy; it wasn't fun. It definitely taught me a lot in terms of just who I was and mind you, this is my mid-twenties. This was between ages Twenty-five to twenty-seven, and I didn't have any responsibilities. You know what I'm saying? It's the same way. It was like I'm the youngest, so my family took care of me. You know, if I called them and say I need money for this, it might take a day, it may take a week, but they're always going to take care of it. And that was the story or the norm, needless to say, for the next like ten years. Because basically, the next ten years were where I battled and struggled and had to deal with a lot of alcohol issues. I don't know. I look at it as that relationship with her; it was something, you know, that I shouldn't have committed myself as a label of like, this is my relationship. I should've never done that. It should've just been like, okay, I'm going to do this for a little while. Not necessarily had to label, but just, you know, be able to wiggle out before that title gets placed.

And I stayed in, stayed in long, and it made for a bad situation, and it made for a rough situation for like the first two years of me being there. The good thing about it is, is that, once I broke away from her, it seemed like when I started dealing with my first fiancé, it was news was getting back to her that I was dealing with this new woman, but it was like, okay, there is no longevity here. It just was a bad situation and a lot of my relationships; I knew that I shouldn't have been in, but I did and alcohol played a role. But I do think that I learned a lot, you know what I'm saying? I learned how to hide alcohol because that's what she did. I don't think I've ever met somebody who honestly hid their alcohol in the freaking bathroom. Like she literally had a full stock bar in her bathroom. But yeah, so I learned how to do that, and I don't know like, that relationship was, it probably should've never started. But I guess I needed the companionship, and that's where it took me.

CHAPTER 4—WOODS

My first engagement was to a woman named Woods. I was working like crazy, substitute teaching full-time, and working a part-time gig in the evenings. It was kind of crazy because the area in where I was teaching, I also briefly went to high school when I was about fifteen. I had this weird feeling I was going to run into somebody from that high school. This particular evening I was working my part-time gig and saw somebody walk by, and I was like, wait a minute, this woman looks familiar. I walked up to her, and I said, "Excuse me, I think I know you."

And she looked at me and she was like, "nah, I don't think so." So, the only thing that really floored her and got her cell phone out was when I said, "Hey, your mom was in *Waiting to Exhale*?"

And then she started asking me questions like, what am I up to? I told her I was teaching and told her this is my second job, got my bachelor's degree, and whatnot. We exchanged numbers, and back then I had one of those rules where it'll be like a two- or three-day grace period before I contact them. And lo and behold, the next day I get a phone call. I think I met her either on a Wednesday or Thursday night. I honestly didn't expect her to call. I probably was just going to wait for the actual weekend, Saturday, Sunday, to reach out to her.

Woods called me that Friday night and I was still dealing with Rossi, you know that very toxic and abusive situation. The conversation was going so well that I almost turned and was heading to see Woods. Instead, I went to the event that night with Rossi, but the whole time I kept thinking about this new woman. I didn't know I was going to run into her. This is before social media was popping off. I think it had just started, but I wasn't into like, searching names and whatever; what it became later as social media began to grow and be able to use it. So, we started dating and, no, I'm sorry, we first started talking and hung out a couple of times, and I think by the second time, I was okay with us hanging out. I went over there and, I was in a wild situation; there was somebody in my life. So, I always travel with protection. But this particular evening, I left my protection in the car because I wasn't necessarily thinking I'm out to get some.

We were watching a movie, drinking some cheap wine when we eventually fell asleep. All of a sudden, this woman was on top of me.

Now mind you, I'm not understanding and knowing what she was referring to at the moment, but what it was is that she wanted the guy that her family had set her up with, retired, Air Force, got a pension, this and this and that. She wanted just the idea of being with a man who already had the security income but wanted to be with a man like myself, who was treating her like she was supposed to be treated. I'll go into that a little bit later because that's what seems to be a problem with a lot of relationships that I was in. Now you're still wondering and caring, trying to figure out what this has to do with alcohol? Well, it has a lot to do with because when I initially was dealing with her, I was drained, but then it was just like with some of the things that I had to go through with her she couldn't make up her mind if she wanted to deal with me or deal with this older guy. But yet, she was still coming to me and then she had all kinds of issues because most of the guys that she dealt with were professional athletes, celebrities and still, she came back to me.

So obviously it wasn't about the money. Eventually, over time I just got rid of all the situations that I was in because we both agreed to commit to one another as far as just dating exclusively. I think that was the worst mistake, but I did it because it just seemed right. Now it's kind of crazy, like I said, we dated for about a year, and it seemed like more or less of a game to where it was like, okay, the relationship was convenient only for her whenever she wanted it. But then she didn't want the relationship, or she wanted to go fuck around and be with these little ballplayers. She knew how to ignore me. But see, I didn't necessarily pick up on it because I was still naive and, I dealt with women that dealt with ballplayers and things of that nature, but those were just pure fucks.

It wasn't anything of trying to secure our relationship , or at least, try to lay the foundation for our future. Like I said, in the relationship, I drank, and a lot of times, we drank together, and it intensified the intimacy. Because as described by her, we were like fucking jackrabbits because that's all we did. And I should've known that it was just a sexual thing, it's not long term, it didn't seem that it was going anywhere. It was like, okay, we have amazing sex, and we'd both be drunk. And then we do that to about one, two o'clock in the morning. I had to go to my job; she had to go to her job, and then we talk about it all day at work.

I think that what really got me is that I had a long-term relationship in Minnesota and when I came to Arizona, it didn't work out between that person and me. That was like, all right, well, maybe this relationship would get me away from infidelity and the party lifestyle and from the lifestyle of multiple women, things of that nature. And so, I proposed to her; now I'm thinking I did it right, I proposed in church. No, that was the biggest mistake. I'm going to tell you why, because I can't remember whether I was going to go to church with her that particular night. I did, then I was like, but I had been drinking all day.

So, I went ahead, you know, it was a night service, and I was just sitting there, and I was like, man, you need to get your life together. If you throw in the towel and just commit yourself to one woman, maybe that'll help you slow down. I mean by slowing down and slowing down to drinking, but in a lot of ways, and my mind was like, am I really ready to commit to being married? Now mind you, this woman had two kids. I didn't mind that. It wasn't an issue that she had two kids; the issue that I eventually had was that she didn't want to be a mother. She wanted to be out in the streets. She wanted to party. She wanted to work hard Monday through Friday. On Saturday she wanted to be in somebody's club or be up under somebody with some money.

And like I said, she didn't have a babysitter, and she had nobody to watch her kids. And then, of course, she'd make me feel bad. There's no telling that she could have been going out with another guy while I'm watching her kids and don't tell him. But the most important, I guess not the most important, but the good thing that came out of that relationship is that I should, well, no, let me stop there. Rewind. Two months later, she found out, well, not even two months after I proposed to her, I'd say about three weeks later, she found out that she was pregnant. We thought it was cool because and like I said, I won't mention names, but I've had some lying ass telling me that they were pregnant and they had an abortion, they had miscarriages and whatnot.

And, I can say it now because I'm out of it, but my question to some of those individuals who told me they were pregnant and told me that they had a miscarriage, was it worth it or was it worth it that you had to sell your soul and pay me for sex? So just want to put it out there. I keep at it. I'm going to try to stay real with this, but that's the truth. So once she found out that she was pregnant, I remember, I never forget the night she went out, then came to my apartment or whatever, and she said she had some margaritas or something and then all of a sudden she was like, well, I don't feel good. Then all of a sudden, she ran to the bathroom; I heard her throwing up. I knocked on the door, asked her, "What's wrong with you?" Woods was like, the only time I throw up is when I'm pregnant. I was like, okay, cool, you know, like I said, I am not tripping because I knew for sure that we had been intimate, and we hadn't been using protection.

So, it was kind of like a catch-22. And you know, I was excited. I'll never forget it. I called my dad that night, and it was devastating because I know that that was the phone call that my dad has been waiting to hear from me saying, 'Hey Dad, my lady, my girlfriend, my wife, my fiancée, whoever it is, is pregnant." But when I told him, I remember, because he was at work, and I'm sure he can if his memory hasn't gone that bad yet. I told him, I said, "Pops, you know the girl I'm dealing with? She told me that she's pregnant." He screams, and I said, "But man, here's the bad news; she doesn't want it." And he was like, why? I was like, well, I, you know, and he's like, well, don't you want it? And I'm like, yes. Then I had to explain to him that I don't believe in abortions. I don't believe in any of that stuff, but it was like, I had no choice. I told him, "Look, man, I'm going to try my best to convince her not to get rid of it." I have my own place, and I even told her, you and your kids can come move in here, and once you have the baby, we can find something that's larger.

She said she was more concerned that she didn't want to be pregnant at the wedding. It was like preserving the life of a child over how you look at a wedding, to me was very heartless, very selfish and just flat out, fucked up. But it was devastating. So, for the next like, give or take, I think about seven days, we went back and forth. I'm like, please, please, please, just don't do it. Whatever it takes, if I have to work three, four, five jobs, I will, but if you get rid of this child, it will devastate me more than you'll ever understand it.

Sure enough, that's what happened. I remember the night before she had already scheduled to get the abortion and like I said, I was dumb, and I was like, well, "Let's just go to the casino, get your mind off of it, and then we'll figure out how you feel in the morning." And so, my dumb ass was like, okay, yeah, let's do it. Despite the fact that I didn't want to, despite the fact that I was not in support of it, I still agreed to it. Not only did I agree to it, but I also paid for it, and that's something that I have to live with for the rest of my life: I paid for an abortion that I wasn't in favor of.

But, what do you do in this situation if a woman doesn't want to have the child when you sit in here like a couple of months before the person found out they were pregnant? Are you going to sit here and have a conversation in terms of how many kids do you want? If you do have a boy, what would you name him? Would they be a third, however it was? And I was just like, wow, you go from talking about that to deciding you want to have an abortion. And so, the day of the abortion, I'll never forget it, was on a Monday, I won't say the month or the year. So, we woke up; I'm at my place; she's at her grandma's house because, at the time, she had given up her apartment to save money, and that's a whole other story. But anyway, so then, that morning and a part of me was like, I didn't want to answer the phone. I didn't want to answer the door. I was just going to just completely, you say you're on your own, but being the nice gentleman that I am, sure enough, I went ahead and agreed to do it, and that was the hard part.

It's just the idea and the fact that I could have

prevented it by not even participating. I could have prevented it by not even answering the call. And, like I said, it still bothers me. There are still times that it seems like I have a dream of a child and it'd be a faceless child, and now that faceless child would be up in age. And it's devastating because there are some people out there that would just lay down every chance they get, and it don't matter how many times they get pregnant, their goal is to get an abortion. And it's like, okay, well those individuals need to hide their dangle two sides. And I'm being honest and I, I don't care at this point, it doesn't matter who I offend, because this is my book.

It's my expressions and feelings. We go into the clinic, and she has the abortion. I will never forget it because the clinic was not too far from one of the hospitals that I had gone into a few times. So, regarding the clinic, there was a lady in there, and this is no joke, she had a baby that was less than a year old and maybe even less than nine months or so, whatever it was. This lady was trying to have an abortion and ask the people to watch her baby while she goes and kills another baby. People were in there with their kids and just had them running around like, wow, okay, these people are not taking this shit seriously.

So, after the abortion procedure went down, being that "good boyfriend," I was hating her at the same time. And then as she's walking out, I'm just like, man, do I run for the hills, get her back to where she needs to go? Or I never talk to this woman again or try to find out what's really going on? And so, of course, I took the other route; I was a good boyfriend. She came, stayed at my place, lied to her family, said that she had to work that day when she wasn't working, got sick, and threw up all over my bedroom floor and all that. I still felt like I needed to be there. I remember that I went and got me like two or three 40-ouncers of malt liquor and got drunk.

I called my sister Quisha. I called my mom, and I was like, what am I supposed to do? It doesn't feel right. I don't know how to feel, what to think at this point because all the other times that women supposedly had abortions and supposedly had miscarriages, somebody's wild woman was ready to have sex, literally the day that they had it. Some of the women I dealt with, it was pretty wild. But I'm not here to tell no lies; it was all truths and facts, and it was hard that for the next nine months: the worst, probably one of the worst moments of my life. But I felt like, I kept asking God, okay God, can you guide me?

God, can you give me whatever sign that you wanted me to see when you had me go with this woman to get that abortion? And I think God was telling me something, but I don't think that I was willing and able to listen to what he had to say and listen to my friends and listen to my family. They all knew that I shouldn't have been in that relationship because that relationship wasn't about love, just lust. At least she trusts somebody enough to watch her kids and still do what she wanted to do and live a life of a single woman and not a life of a mother of two kids who just killed the third one. So, I mean, I drink; I drank before we got engaged, but I drank more during that period after the abortion. We were still engaged, and I was in between jobs.

I wasn't making any money, so when I came upon a little bit of change, the only thing she thought about was how she could spend it. But mind you, she was making money. Mind you, one of her baby daddies was an attorney, so she was getting a nice amount in child support. So, I couldn't deal with it, it was like, dang, I finally had an opportunity to know that, okay, I'm a father and can't nobody tell me otherwise because I saw the pregnancy test and it said pregnant. The only thing is I didn't know if it was mine, even to this day, I don't know. But I still feel like heck; I did have sex with her. I did have unprotected sex regardless of how many other women I've had unprotected sex with, and none of them have ever been pregnant.

So, it was devastating. Even to this day, some ten plus years ago, it still affects me. I had to forgive but never forget. But I was just like, why, we are about to get married, but the relationship after the abortion was weird. I had the paperwork, what the doctor said as far as how the woman's supposed to take care of her body after the abortion. And I don't know if that stuff makes you like hornier or more aroused, but like the moment that she knew that she could have sex again, she was ready to do it. We had sex a couple of times, and she didn't get pregnant.

The next nine months weren't easy because, in the back of my mind, I didn't trust her. I wasn't perfect, and I was drinking. I had women on the side, and they knew that I was engaged, but didn't care because they just wanted to have sex with me. It's not to make myself look good, but it's really what happened. A lot of women did a lot of dirt to me, and it was like, okay, well, these women are now back in my life. It got to the point where I had these women paying me for sex. This is no joke.

Woods's family loved me even though I might not have had that top secure, high paying job, but they knew they saw the potential. I was trying to better myself. It was just that I was in bad situations that made it harder and tougher for me to get ahead. And a lot of times I put my pride, sometimes I put some pussy, put a lot of things on hold for me not to get what I wanted to get out of life. And when I think, that's another reason why I struggled and battled with alcoholism in my twenties. It was like I busted my ass to continue college, hoping that, okay, I got this bachelor's degree, then not be able to get work. It was the exact opposite. It was like, I got a degree, but I can't find a single job that wanted to pay me something more than seven or eight an hour.

So, it's the same, but that's just the nature of the beast. We went on trips, you know, we pretended like we were really in love with each other. I was in love with her, but I was more or less in love with her physicality and not the inner spirit. Then a particular incident happened. I'll never forget it. I won't say the company I was working for, but this particular day I decided, you know, I woke up. We were living together at the time.

During this duration of me and her being together, I had two apartments, one with her and myself and one that was by myself. I maintained two apartments for like three months without even working a full-time job and not doing anything illegal. And that's on record too. This particular day, I remember it was a Friday she just came out and she just flat out told me she don't think she could marry me because I don't ever have any money and I was always going to my family borrowing money. And I was like, ain't this about a bitch? And I said it to myself, and I was like, okay when I had thousands upon thousands in my bank account, you weren't concerned about that. When I had thousands upon thousands of dollars in my account, you wanted to go to Vegas. You weren't worried about that. When I had thousands upon thousands of dollars, we went somewhere.

We had gone to this resort South of Tucson. She wasn't worried about that then; you know what I'm saying? And it was like, okay, but now that my money didn't run out, I'm going on trips, I'm paying for kids' dinners and taking her out to plus restaurants and all this stuff. She felt, okay, well I done got everything I can out of this man. So, I went to work. The worst mistake, I should have called her out that day. I drank all day and let's just say that it wasn't the right thing to do. And I drove home, according to what my car looked like when I crashed into something; to this day, I still don't know what I crashed into.

I went home. By this time, it was like five or six, and I just got into it with her, just went off. She called the police and lied and said that I didn't live there, but yet if a man didn't live there, why am I paying half the rent? Why are my clothes in there? Why are my shoes here and everything else? But most of everything in the place was hers because I got rid of all my furniture before I decided to move in. So yeah, that was pretty much it. So, she basically told the police I didn't live there, so the police told me I had to leave. That's what I did. I left, went to Circle K; it wasn't too far, and then I got me something to drink on top of my being already drunk.

Now mind you, I don't know how long it was, but just know that I was somewhere, and I messed around, and I got drunk, went home, went back to the apartment. I tore that apartment up, punched a hole in the door, all because it was like well into like nine months' worth of hell that this woman put me through. And then I finally just got fed up, and that's the problem that I had that I didn't know. It was like that anger, that hatred, that frustration, that violent, that person wasn't really who I was. But it was because like, I had endured so much pain in that relationship. It showed and so, yeah, I got arrested. Yeah, I got a misdemeanor. Yeah, I did sixteen hours. Yeah, I lost my job, and I was homeless.

CHAPTER 5—PATRICE

Patrice is a great woman that I hold near and dear in my heart to this day. We met back when I was substitute teaching in Minnesota. I was in a situation that I was comfortable in. But when Patrice and I met, we clicked instantly. We hung out a few times, nothing sexual, just great company, and conversation. She was different from what I was used too. That's why I probably didn't really try to get involved because I just knew how my mentality was at that time (wild). I kept in contact with her for years, and by this time, I was in the Army, and she was there for me through some really difficult times. We gave a long-distant relationship a try. Was it tough? Yes! But throughout that entire time, I was hiding so much. I loved her and cared a lot about her, but I hid how severe my drinking was. Little did she know I still had my addiction to alcohol. I wanted to be in a relationship with Patrice and didn't necessarily know how to really deal with one, just getting out of one relationship in 2008 that saw me lose a lot of stuff, place to live, arrested, and the list went on and on.

And during that time, she came to visit me two times, had a ball, showed her around the area, went out to eat in the city of Fayetteville, North Carolina. But I was still me hiding the fact that I had this issue, which was drinking and of us dating, I would say not even seven months. Like, because we knew each other for so long, I was just like, man, you know, why not? And sure enough, like I came back to visit and had it all planned out. I hired my buddy as a photographer, picked a location in St. Paul, took pictures, and then eventually proposed in the middle of the photoshoot.

Then things took a turn for the worse. A day or two later, we go to a 4th of July function at my sister's house. With tons of alcohol around, I made a fool of myself. I drank a lot because my sister and my brother-in-law, they probably still do have it, they had a full- full- full-blown bar. And what I mean by full-blown it was everything you can think of as far as hard liquor, everything you could think of as far as beer. I can't remember if there was any wine, but I'm pretty sure it was there. And I just remember going downstairs in the basement, and I think my brother had come down there and was like, man, you got to slow down. And I'm just like to hell with this, you know, I was celebrating my birthday for one. Two, I came home on vacation. It was one of my first road trips since I was in the Army. But I still had other pain that I was dealing with and probably wasn't a good idea to drink. So somehow or another, like from what I remember, I got into it with both of my brothers and they followed me like a whole block, and I was just going off cussing them out, swinging, whatever. But they didn't fight back, and I guess, Patrice and they're both like, man, you got to take him somewhere. He just can't stay here. I end up at Patrice's place. I threw up all over her new comforter set and the floor. I drank so much, I slept all day, and I can't remember if it was like a Saturday. It had to be a Saturday because I was able to get alcohol.

And, I remember, because at the time she was living on the North side of Minneapolis. And I remember walking there, it might've been like a mile and a half, two miles, and it was so funny that actually where I was walking to was close to the very first treatment facility that I was in. And don't ask me how I could remember how to get back to her house, but I was able to, and I think I ended up buying like two tall cans or some kind of malt liquor that was over 8%. I'm just walking down the street drinking, not a single cop in sight. I have been cited for open container, they could have arrested me on-site, but none of that happened. And so, I get back there, and I guess she kind of was just like, well man, I can't take care of you. You got to go somewhere. It was crazy because we were going on a trip to Kansas City like a couple of days after that, and we still went. And little did she know that I would tell her I was going to the store to get tobacco, but I really wasn't. I was going to, like, it was either a Circle K or QT or something, some store, but it became a favorite store, and I would just get something to drink. And that was the only way for me to function. That entire trip is that I had to have some type of alcohol, and she probably knew about it but didn't say anything. And it was crazy because we had a good time. We went around at various landmarks in Kansas City, Missouri, and in Kansas City, Kansas. And we never talked about it. And to this day we never really, really, really addressed it, to the point where it's like, okay, look, you did this. I can't deal with that. You know, I eventually found out, I guess through a conversation from my mom, she told me what was going on and how alcohol has affected her family. And she just said that she couldn't go down that road again. And so, I, and like I said, I didn't find that out for years after.

Basically, after we came back from Kansas City, I think I saw her a couple of times and whatnot, but it just still wasn't the same. And so, like I'm boarding the plane now going back to North Carolina and didn't know what was going to happen. I proposed to her; she had the ring. I'm like, okay, we can work through it. And you know, she told me you know, you need to get yourself together. So, I think I volunteered to go to this alcohol substance class or classes, which was like a weeklong. And in a lot of ways it was like, I think, I was doing it to get out of work because I didn't want to really be doing this work as a cook anymore. But so, I did it. I got out of work for five days, and that was my, that was my duty station, you know, or place of duty for those five days.

And so, I'd probably say about a week or two after that, she didn't tell me. She didn't say anything. She just sent me it was a priority mail letter, I think, and all the things you had in there was a ring, and then all she said was cash the ring in and buy a car. Not saying, you know, she never necessarily said like, okay, the relationship is over or anything like that. So, you know, yeah, I was devastated because, for one, I embarrassed myself, but for two, it's like, dang, okay, not again. You know, I was already engaged once; that engagement led me to jail for a night. The second time, I should have gone to jail, but I didn't, and now I'm losing somebody that was really a good person, true to the heart. And it affected me, and it was to the point where I didn't know what to do.

I didn't think that I'd ever get in a relationship again because of my track record of having two failed engagements within two years, and there was no end in sight. It was like, okay, I'm in this military career per se, but not really and truly wanting to be there. So, it was like I was almost sabotaging my own career, but I don't think people really understand like what it was I was going through. What really triggered me and got me to the point where I had to take a drink, and not just one, I had to drink malt liquor for a start and then close the night out with something hard. And eventually, that led to a lot of years of struggling with the addiction to alcohol. So of course, when she sent me the ring back, you know, I'm sure I contacted somebody in my family, probably my mom, if not my sister, maybe both.

And I started to drink again, and it was heavy because I'm just like, man, like I can't get anything right. I continuously get the same results. And so, then this is where my ex-wife kind of came into the picture, but see my ex-wife was plotting and planning this because she did the same thing when my first engagement failed. She's calling me, you know, telling me about how she's in a bad relationship with her baby daddy and whatnot. And then it seemed like the setup because the same thing happened, and I was very vulnerable. I was in a state of mind where like, hell, I probably would have married a tree. You know what I'm saying? That's just how bad it was because, you know, here it is she's showing me the right amount of attention. She's calling me, she's texting me, whatever. I can't remember if we were emailing each other back then, but the communication was there, and that's all I needed was somebody to listen. God knows what she was doing in the interim, you know, she was in Arizona, I was in North Carolina.

So, this chapter is not necessarily focused on my ex-wife, but it's about the relationship with Patrice. And the reason being is because I thought that she and I would never talk again. And I remember she called me right around my birthday to wish me a happy birthday. I'd never forgotten it. She called me to say a happy birthday. I was like, please get me out of this marriage. I don't want to be with her. I said, I will file these divorce papers right now if you give me another chance. That didn't happen, but it was my heart, and I'll never forget it because I had gone to the store, you know, got me a bottle of something to drink, and I didn't go into my neighborhood. I parked my car on the street going into the neighborhood before the cul-de-sac.

I'm sitting out there, and I guess my ex-wife or whatever, she was like Ken is taking a long time just to go to the store, you know because like I said, she knew my movements and knew how long it would take me. So, then she started walking, so she saw me out there on the phone, and probably figured it out because she always like, loved to Snoop and go through my phone and she probably found out eventually who I was talking to. So that was her main threat, you know, was my second fiancé. She was really, really, and truly threatened because she knew how much I really cared about her, and now she can throw it in her face like, okay, I'm married to him. We got, you know, all this stuff, because I'm still to this day, don't know how she found out that we had got married because we were, we were friends on Facebook, and then I guess she deleted me or whatever. And maybe it was her sister; I don't know. But somebody told her I had got married based on social media.

And so, for a while, I didn't talk to her. Occasionally I shoot her an email; I'll just be like, hey, how are you doing, you know, just letting you know I'm still alive. You know, she would ask me about married life, and in a lot of ways, I had to be honest because it wasn't something that I knew I shouldn't have been in. It was abusive from the start to the end. And in 2019 it's still, you know, she thinks she has the power, but she doesn't. But I'm not going to lie to you; out of all the women I've dealt with, like she's literally in the top two or three. And I won't place it because I don't need anybody to be jealous, but this is my book. So, in a lot of ways, anybody could be that number one. But she's the one; I believe she got away with the best heart and had the true best interest of me.

Like I said over the years, we keep in contact with each other and for a minute, like I never saw her. It was more or less like, okay, I am going to shoot her an email even though she's had the same phone number for probably as long as I've known her. I couldn't bring myself to call her and something told me like, okay, like I said, we kept in contact over the years, all the way up until the present day. But it was just interesting because like, I had reached out to her when I moved back to Minnesota in 2016

November, and we didn't hang out probably till about four months later.

It could have been like, on some reality TV, like, let me throw some water at you or whatever she drinks or throw food at me. But then she was like, look this is six, seven years later. And she was just like, I don't really want to talk about that. It's in the past. Let's move on, you know, let's just, you know, how are you doing the day? And when she said that, it was just like, of course, she's a beautiful woman. And a part of me was just like, man, the attraction was, you know, it'll always be there.

You know she's beautiful inside now. And for me it was like, all right, well shoot, should I try to holler at her or not? So, we didn't necessarily, you know, we never had, even to this day; we've never had anything since 2010. It's all just been hanging out. We go out to eat; we go to dinner. She, you know, she came through in 2018 for my graduation party, which I thought was really cool. And she's truly been there for me as a real strong support system. Make sure that my health is good. You know, like we went on a trip together to DC and I had got sick when I was out there, like really sick. My blood sugar, the levels were like 50 and 60 or something. It was low and I didn't know what to do because it was like I'm taking this medication, but my blood sugar levels were just way too low. And I think it was because, for one, it was hot. It was really hot in DC those two or three days, three days that we were there, it was extremely hot. I mean, I should've been drinking more than just water, and eventually, I figured it out. Got Gatorade, you know, but still, I couldn't, I couldn't manage it. Like I'd be up all night sweating, whatever. And you know, we shared a room, two separate beds and you know, I couldn't tell her the truth. Like, man, I'm really over here struggling. And we talked about it and you know, the reason I'm solely giving her a chapter is because I think I gained more respect for her at the airport. We got to the airport and then she was just like, it seemed like she had something on her mind or her plate, and then suddenly she was just like, what were your intentions on this trip?

I don't know if, because you know, I am not going to say always, but you know, sometimes you just carry protection. You never know when you in situations like this. So, I had some condoms, and she probably saw it in the bag or whatever. And then she was just like, you know, I, you know, did you think something was going to happen? I was like, man, shoot, I don't know. You know, but if it was, I'll be prepared. And then she was like, you know, what we had was good, and it didn't end well, but I've earned a lot of respect for you. And I'm not like these other bitches that ever hurt you. I genuinely care about you, and I care about your health and your well-being and things of that nature.

And I was just like, wow, I felt bad because a part of me was like, you know, I'm not trying to, you know, lose the friendship of a good person. And they say that men and women can't be friends, but you can. But we just had to talk about it. And after she said what she said, you know, I told her, I said, look man, I fucked up. I know that I did some stupid shit in 2010. And those stupid things that I did ended our relationship, but at least it didn't end the friendship because we are still friends to this day. We don't talk longer than four days; somebody is texting me just to make sure we are straight. And I was just the respect that I have for her.

I mean I have a lot of friends that I've met along the way, some that I dated and some that I never dated, but it just seems like even if I wanted to get rid of her, I can't. We just formed that bond and it's like I said, it's not anything sexual, and there's no relationship going on, you know, it's just pure friendship and just making sure that you know, each other's good. And like I said, she supports me, just like she's a part of the family in terms of my sobriety and she knows that it's difficult. If I have days I struggle, I go to her and I say, "Hey look, this is what's going on." And she's like, okay well I'm going to pray for you. And then usually the prayer that she puts in front of me eventually comes to fruition.

And this is not just one time. This has been numerous, numerous times. And I'm just like, wow, you know, and you know for that I just, you know, I told her, I said that you're stuck with me for the rest of my life. And if I die before you die, I will be your guardian angel, and I will protect you. And I mean that because there's a lot of things that she didn't have to do. And like I said, they're not, at least the women I've come across, they're not too many like that. And hopefully that when that day does come that, you know, she gets in a relationship; hopefully, that guy will recognize how good she is because she's a good person. And so, it's tough. You know, people are going to look at this chapter and saying, hmm, you're in a relationship, but you're talking about another woman.

But she's definitely one of my best friends. And, I say that because she's known me for a very long time and eventually my new lady is going to have to meet her because I'm not going to break this friendship, not for her or anybody else. So, I just wanted to make sure that I emphasized that she's still a really good person and regardless if there was an engagement in sexual relationship. And like I said, you know, my family, they, you know, see her as family whenever she comes around. She doesn't have to be up underneath me. I don't have to be up underneath her, and she could still have a good time. And that's one thing that I like, and she can really cook. Oh, my goodness, banana pudding, top dollar. I'm going just to say that, put that out there.

But yes, I am blessed and very thankful for the one God did bring into my life. I thank God for taking her out of my life for that time. And then when she came back into my life when I was just like, I don't want to be married. And she was well, I hope and pray that things get better. I'm like, am not shit getting better, okay because that's just how bad the relationship was. So, I'm very thankful and blessed to have good people, good support. Good support regardless of if it's somebody that I dated or somebody I was engaged to, even though I was only engaged twice and then just got married because I wasn't engaged to my ex-wife, we just got married. But you know I'm blessed and happy. It's not too often you can come across really and truly good people.

And I'm happy that she's a friend and she's a part of it. And it's always encouraging. It's always positive. You know, even if she got personal problems, it's very rare that she'll tell me. Sometimes I'll pry it out of her, but that's kind of what friends are for, because it's not all about me, it's about her too. So, I just wanted to say a big thank-you to Patrice for being a dear friend, being my bestie. And I would honestly say truly know who I am as a person, especially the good, I mean, she knows the bad side, but she knows that I also have a good heart until the next chapter. It's getting better. It's getting better.

CHAPTER 6—MARRIAGE FACES

It was 2003; I just graduated with my bachelor's degree. My brother Anthony bought me a plane ticket to Phoenix for a few weeks. The day after arriving, we hit the road and went to Las Vegas for a family reunion for the woman he was dating at the time, who is now his ex-wife. I will never forget when I met Nichele. She was cute, thick, light skin, but I was in a relationship and had no desire at that time to talk to her in that way.

I noticed a pattern over the years with Nichele. Each time I got out of an engagement, she was always reaching out. So, in a lot of our conversations, I found myself venting about my past. I was trying to figure out why this woman was interested in me, knowing that I was weak, vulnerable, and lonely. Not knowing that there was a lot of baggage that came with her, I kind of put it to the side because I wanted a relationship. I wanted just to have the title of saying I'm married, this is my wife, and not really understanding everything else that came with it. I came back to Phoenix for the first time in almost two and a half years after my arrest in 2008. I didn't expect or anticipate being in a relationship with her, and I felt like, okay, I'm doing this, but it's all for the wrong reasons. I'm doing this not because I'm in love with this woman because I wasn't in love with her when I got married. I was drunk, and I decided, yeah, okay, let's go ahead and do it. I didn't understand what lay ahead.

Why am I doing this? Is this for the right reasons? She got married to run away from what she was dealing with in Phoenix. I was getting married. It was just like, okay, well, somebody wants to marry me but looking back at it now, some I guess you can say eight years later. It's like, wow, I don't think I would have ever done that with a sober mind that I currently have now. We got married at a courthouse in Raleigh, North Carolina; it was April 8, 2011. We didn't have any witnesses, so we got two people.

Nichele found two people that were walking out who just got a divorce. The guy had the same first name as mine, Kenneth, that was interesting, and we did it anyway. That Friday evening, we had dinner, returned to the hotel. Instead of going inside the hotel. I decided to stay in the car and smoke a cigar. So I called my sister Quisha and told her I was drunk.

She asked, "What did you do?" I was just like, nothing! She then replied, "I feel like you did something." She knows me very well.

I eventually told my family months later, I was already married, and it didn't come as a surprise to any of them. I can remember during that time when we first got married; I was still going through my issues with alcohol, still having these inner demons of an abortion from my first engagement. My failed first engagement, failed second engagement, and now married. Just not with the person I wanted to be with but yet and still I got married anyway. And let me tell you like that marriage wasn't easy. We were married from 2011 to 2017—living together five of the six years.

I'm only going to pinpoint a few stories because I could write a book on just that marriage alone. My struggles with alcoholism didn't start with that marriage; it tested my character at home and work. Even though I was married, I was still in love with another woman. That woman was Patrice. I remember on my birthday, August 2, 2011, I called Patrice and told her I was willing to go AWOL to get out of that marriage and to be with her. That's just how serious I was, but she wasn't trying to hear it. Patrice wasn't trying to have anything to do with what I was saying, but it was a truth, and it was from the heart.

I knew in my mind that I truly didn't want to be married to Nichele. But I was married and now had to deal with it. Plus, I was now able to move out of the barracks. Staying in the barracks was like reliving college again. I didn't have to worry about people coming into your room at any time. All I had to do was get married, and that problem would be eliminated. I will say that we both had vices; we both had addictions. Her addiction was a casino, and mine was drinking. Putting those two things together was a big fucking problem.

Her addiction outweighed mine at times because in a lot of ways, it was money that was being lost and blamed on me. In reality, it was her spending it but tried to blame me and say that I did it or I was drunk and wasn't thinking or so on. Nichele couldn't go to the casino after she moved to North Carolina with me because there wasn't one. The closest casino was like four or five hours from Fayetteville going towards West Virginia.

I recall an instance with her drug dealer, baby daddy. CPS left a message on my voicemail. I was on day five in the field training with the Army. I called them back, and the lady asked me some personal questions regarding my then stepdaughter: had I ever seen her naked, ever touched her inappropriately, and so on. I called my ex, and she told me CPS also left her a voicemail. Nichele was headed to Atlanta to party. I asked her to come back, and she refused. So my supervisor let me leave the field early to tend to the matter. I called again and begged her to come back from Atlanta. Still, the answer was no, and I drank the entire weekend away. Nichele returned that Monday, and I let her have it. I went off on her and told her to call the bastard. We spoke, but it was a waste of time. Weeks went by, still no response from CPS. All of a sudden, she tells me that I was cleared of the accusations. The baby daddy called my ex and her mother to apologize but wasn't man enough to call me. The sad part about that man is that he deals drugs out of his mama's house where she runs a day care. I hope that house is raided.

The relationship was one-sided; she only cared about her family and friends in Phoenix over anything else. My family wasn't of any importance for us to see them. But we had to make it a point to be somewhere in Arizona for somebody's function. If it was a birthday, wedding, or graduation party, we were in attendance—did none of those when they came to my family. So now you see where I'm going at with this story. But yeah, there were a lot of times a lot of just weird stuff that was going on. You know, there were times where I'm stuck at home watching her kids while she was in the streets doing God knows what with God knows who.

This was a person who will complain every chance she got about the fact that I was drinking yet encouraged it at the same time. We would go to the liquor store, and she would be like, don't you want anything to drink? So, I'm like, make up your mind. Either you want me to drink, or you don't. There was stuff that she would post on social media that was negative about me, my family, so of course, I would get drunk, talk about her, her family, and friends. I had no filter at all nor cared who was reading it. Our relationship was based on social media. And so many people got involved, and so many people had their opinion, and frankly, I didn't care.

I got into a lot of trouble with my subordinates, but they also respected me because of my work performance when I was at work, and it's not so much that I hid the idea I was an alcoholic. Because some people could smell it because in a lot of ways I drank until one, two o'clock in the morning and had to be at work in a few hours. So, it was one of those things, I mean, I'm not going to lie to you. I learned a lot. I made some good relationships with people, and some relationships I regret ever confiding in. But that's just the nature of the beast of being in the military that you just don't know who you can honestly and really trust until you get into a conflict with people. And looking back on it now, hindsight is twenty-twenty, because a lot of people that was hating on me, now respect me. Because they see what I've come from in terms of the mistakes that I made as far as my alcoholism getting into trouble and getting away with things and now, they see that my life is totally different.

I remember one time I punched a hole in the door while using the bathroom. Nichele was talking shit like always; in doing so, it made me extremely upset. I will admit I was drinking, but I like my privacy when using the bathroom. Right before we moved out of the military housing and heading to Texas for my next duty station, I had swung and hit the chair up against the wall, and like, damaged so bad; of course, they charged me a couple hundred bucks, but I think the problems truly started to grow and manifest once we got to El Paso because it was just a lot of things that she was doing that just wasn't it just didn't add up. Every time I would check our bank account, there was a withdrawal for $100. There was a withdraw for $200. She would always say oh, this is money I needed for food but then she would swipe her debit card to get food, so it was like okay, which one is it. I later figured out where the money was going, and it was the casino.

In 2013 we had relocated to El Paso. I would say probably like about January, February timeframe from driving cross country, which was very difficult driving two vehicles, my car and her car separately. It should have been an initial road trip for me to kind of plan out what I was going to do, as far as myself, as far as my health, as far as alcoholism, my marriage, but I guess I wasn't necessarily focused on that. I was more or less concerned about when's the next stop in terms of when I can go get me something to drink. I'm sad to say it, but it's the truth. So I remember getting to El Paso we didn't have a place to stay because we were like number 100 and something on the waiting list. Then I don't know, somehow it got changed, and we were able to move in actually to a new housing development on base, which was cool, really nice, and everything.

And I remember this was like maybe when I first started in processing, I had met this guy named Griff. He and I are still cool to this day, so I big shout out to him. Hopefully, he's doing well. Last time I talked to him, he was working on sobriety, so maybe I should call him and check on him. So, despite my having a receding hairline, I still would let my hair grow. My ex-wife, at that time we were still married, decided to go to Arizona by herself. I forgot why I wasn't able to go, but she went. And so, I was bored; I think it was like a Friday night, you know, I'm having a couple of drinks and playing music. And then I just cut my hair, and I had been toying with it like I was going to cut it all off, but I just wasn't ready to let what was left of my hair go. And I can remember posting a picture on social media and basically getting a shock response from a lot of people because people had been used to seeing me with hair. Everybody was welcoming and receptive to the idea of me cutting my hair. It was kind of like, okay, I'm at a new city and state, new duty station, you know, can make some changes. But my ex-wife didn't like it, didn't like the comments, didn't like my friends commenting on the picture, didn't like my family commenting on the picture.

As far as like, other issues in the marriage I mentioned in the first part of this, you know, finances were always an issue. It was like one person was trying to get out of debt, usually would be me, and then it would be her constantly trying to stay in debt, if not create more debt. There were a lot of times when two, three, four, and $5,000 would come in the account in terms of school or taxes, and tax returns. And it was always, oh yeah, I'm going to get out of debt. But in reality, she blew all that money in the casino. It's strange and how you can have a marriage with two people who both have addictions, yet yours is the problem. I'm not saying that alcoholism is any better than being a person who gambles, but I know one thing that gambling, losing hundreds and thousands of dollars, failing to report it on your taxes, things of that nature, having to get audited, then you have to come out and pay. So, there were many things that could have spiraled out and got worse if I hadn't been paying attention or just so happened to check the mail.

I should have gotten out of when a lot of these red flags were there, but I didn't, you know what I'm saying? Like, I told you, I can't sit here and say that I was a perfect man in my marriage because there were times where, you know, I felt the neglect or as that she didn't want to be bothered with me or no intimacy and doing things that I wasn't supposed to, you know, even though I got caught. She probably didn't care because she was doing the same thing if not worse, but it was just more or less the conversation, talking to people just getting off whatever, you know is on my mind or my heart for that particular day and moment. And there were a lot of women there for me.

Was it appropriate? No, it definitely wasn't appropriate, but when you're married and the person you're with doesn't want to do anything intimately, with you and is holding out for forty-five to sixty days with no sex. And if not longer than that and won't touch you won't be affectionate, sometimes it happens that way. I'm not perfect; needless to say, I'm not a perfect person. And I wasn't perfect in the marriage. You know, like I said, I knew that I didn't really want to be in the military. I think that it's kind of enhanced, it made my decision a lot easier when I got married because I started to see the things that it was like, okay, well I got to do this for her. I got to do this for her kids, or I got to do this for her family. But then it was never anything about like, what is it that I can do for myself? What is it that I can do to improve my health? What is it that I can do so that I can stop drinking? These are the type of things that I should have been looking at. But I was just, like I said before, just in love with the idea of being married. In love with the idea of saying, hey, like, oh my wife, but them not knowing that it was the worst situation in a lot of ways. I didn't want to go home. And I don't know, I can't remember if I've mentioned it in the other chapter, but I will say that it's unfortunate that looking back on the marriage as a whole overall in terms of the form of control.

The arguments seemed to get worse; this was when the police started to get involved more, coming to the house. She would call every chance she would get, not knowing that this would hinder or hurt my career. I'd have to answer to my chain of command about something that happened on the weekend. Going in front of my superiors and explaining I was drinking would lead to us getting into it. To my unit, I was labelled a drunk. July 2014, her life changed; she got arrested for domestic violence. As of right now, her nursing license is probably in question, because she shouldn't be even practicing nursing or working in the medical field for that arrest that she got. I was a fool for not pressing charges. Hindsight being 20/20, Nichele will always have that misdemeanor on her record and won't be able ever to practice nursing. She can only perform administrative work.

With that domestic violence charge, my unit forced me to go to treatment in Alexandria, Virginia, and I had to do thirty days of lockdown. I felt like I was in jail or a halfway house, and she didn't make it any easier. She wasn't supportive, she didn't care, she didn't really empathize with the fact that she's the one that got me there. That thirty days was hell! I stayed in a lockdown ward at this hospital. I had to be in uniform most of the time because that was considered my duty station. Since my unit shipped me off to treatment, I had to cancel my trip to Minnesota for my birthday. I was blamed for the whole ordeal, and they were getting ready to kick me out. At this point, I didn't care about her or the Army for that matter. I was directed not to drink. You think I followed those orders? Hell no! I drank even more. When it came time to evaluate my performance, my personnel file had nothing in it. I call that an act of GOD. Instantly I knew it was time to get out the Army. I went ahead and made a doctor's appointment and made sure I put in for the medical discharge because, at this point, I was embarrassed. There was no sense of me being in this unit or staying in the Army. I'm walking around like a zombie. Not really working, just at home drinking and waiting for the day I will be let go from the Army.

Months before I got out of the Army, she went behind my back and decided to start the process of getting a house. She had my credit ran without my permission to get approved for a loan. Her credit was bad, so she wasn't able to be on the loan. I opened a bank account and added her to it. I deposited $500. I had a bad feeling about the house after seeing the place. I spoke with my sister Quisha, and she suggested we rent a property for a year cause she felt the marriage was beyond repair. I actually listened and decided not to go thru with the house after all. I lost $1,200 of the earnest money, but we weren't ready for owning a home. Nichelle was devastated and spent that $500. I found a house to rent and put up the deposit. She wasn't happy, but I preferred our own place than staying in her parents' tiny home.

I made the mistake of going back to Arizona, August 2015. I was on her home field, she had the home field advantage and trust me, I felt it. I had married a fucked-up person that really cared about herself and not even the kids that she birthed. She didn't care. It was all about going to the clubs and blowing money at the casino. Nichele was a functioning alcoholic because there were hidden bottles and all kinds of stuff around the house. Nichele's mom was an alcoholic, so I believe that is where it came from. I didn't want to work, just put my mind on something different. She wasn't in favor of me going back to finish my master's program. I worked two jobs, but neither lasted longer than three weeks. So most of my free time was dedicated to drinking. I was trying to process what just happened during my Army career. Adjusting to being a civilian was difficult, especially when I was used to structure. Now I had the freedom to do what I wanted.

Alcohol took over my life. I was drinking from sunup to sundown and most of the night. I began having stomach issues. It started off feeling like cramps, which lead to feeling like somebody hit my stomach with a baseball bat. It was so bad that I wasn't able to get out the bed. I eventually went to the emergency room. I was diagnosed with pancreatitis and was hospitalized for nine days. I thought I was going to die. Nichele wasn't really there for me during that time. She would come to visit, stay no more than an hour, and after that, I was left alone. I gained close to thirty pounds in the first couple of days. My stomach was blocking all liquids from the IV. And magically, I lost that weight plus ten more. I was released and still wanted to drink. Nichele left me days after I got out of the hospital. Dark days were ahead of me.

My birthday was here, Mom in town helping me pack up the house. Ding Dong! Nichele at the door with the police. I went off on her and the police. Told them to get the fuck off the property. She wanted the cable box; little did she know the cable was in my name. A few weeks later, we had to be out of the house since the lease was up. She didn't help me clean cause she was upset I took most of the stuff and put it in storage. I was able to swindle the owner to send her the deposit. August 31, 2016, was the last time I saw Nichelle. Thank God!

Looking back on the marriage, I'd be a fool to say there weren't fun times, yes it was, but the bad outweighs the good. We didn't trust each other, let alone really, truly, wholeheartedly, love each other. This was just something to do, and it was like either this will work, or we need to go our separate ways. But I think that the ultimate goal is that we both knew that we probably were not going to. We're probably both surprised that it made it as long as it did. I'm glad that it's over. I'm glad that chapter in my life is complete because it was doomed from the start.

CHAPTER 7—SPONSOR–SPIRITUAL FACES

My sponsor Marie is an 84-year-old lady from Poland. She has been my sponsor since 2008, when I came back to Minnesota after getting arrested. Those first few months of going to AA, I was for sure entering those doors drunk. I didn't want to be there. I was more or less there because my mom forced me to be there. I listened but still didn't think I had a problem. The one thing I couldn't figure out is why the woman was so concerned with me being sober. Marie has been sober for over thirty-five years. So she clearly knows what she is talking about. Even when I joined the Army, my mom would tell me that she asked about me.

While in AA, I did more listening than participating cause I felt I didn't have a problem. But Marie was always right there telling me, "Keep coming back." Despite doing the alcohol programs with the Army, it didn't feel the same way as it did going to my home AA group in Minnesota. Once I decided to move back to Minnesota, I knew once sober where I would be a couple times a week. Since I lived an hour and fifteen minutes away, I only went to a few meetings a month. I can't say I followed the 12 Steps in a particular order but did them (and still do) a few times over during my sobriety journey. Some are not a fan of AA for whatever reason. But it's the people in those meetings I grew to know, and they got to know me.

Over time I grew more comfortable with sharing my past and all that was going on. I found the support I was once ignoring years prior. I took to heart what was being shared in the room. It made me feel that I wasn't alone in my path to sobriety. Some had day, weeks, months, and years sober. I could think about whether I was mentally tough enough to stick to a life of sobriety. When I started celebrating my sobriety months, I was like wow! You might be on to something. Marie would always tell me, "Keep it Simple." I didn't understand that at first. Only control what you have power over. Try not to save the world and yourself all in one day. I follow that saying daily.

Marie has been a sponsor for over ten years. Despite being sober for only three-plus years of that, I was never judged. She just wanted to see me sober and away from those that led or kept me in a drunken state of mind. Marie is a phone call/text message away. I am greeted from time to time with so many encouraging messages. It's almost like Marie can tell when something is wrong. I will get a random text at a moment when I'm going thru some tough situations, and we will talk. The advice given is always on point, and I appreciate her for that.

I went back to Minnesota this past Christmas, 2019. Marie was so upset that the location where AA was held, no longer held meetings. She didn't get the chance to present me with my three-year sober coin as she did on my first day, one year, and two years sober. I called her to set up a date for us to meet, and I drove over to her house. Marie gave me a stuffed frog with a coin around its neck. This was the first time I can remember getting a stuffed animal, and I wasn't embarrassed. I have the frog sitting next to my TV as a constant reminder of the long journey

I took to get sober and the good people who love and support my sobriety. Marie, I Love You and appreciate what you have done for me over the years.

Reverend Patterson, where do I start? When you moved up to Minnesota, Pops said we have a cousin up here and has his own church. This was 2004; life in alcohol wasn't a problem. My problem was how I was feeling having a college degree and still struggling to find a solid career. So, I joined the New Hope Baptist Church, got baptized, and thought I was ready to give my life to God. I was still in the streets, having fun like any other man in his mid-twenties. I moved to Arizona in 2005, and Patterson told me to keep in touch. I held him to that.

My life was in shambles; I reached a level of no return with alcohol. He continued to pray for me. Fast forward three years later. I'm back in Minnesota, deep into alcohol; Patterson set up an appointment for me to go to treatment in North Minneapolis. I felt set up by Pops, his third wife, and Patterson. So, for some time, I didn't contact him. But when I got married, Patterson saw my life taking a downward spiral. I began to call him more because I was upset with God. Why me? Why did I deserve what I went through in my marriage? He flat out told me you need to find a woman who you are equally yoked with.

I was happy to call him and let him know about Whitney. This past Christmas (2020), I went to church while in Minnesota. In the middle of the sermon, he called me up to give a mini testimony. It felt good to share some of my struggles from the past. Thank-you, New Hope Baptist Church for always keeping me in prayer. Patterson, I want to apologize for calling you when I was drunk. But that storm has passed, and I walk a different path. Thanks for the prayers and for never giving up on me.

CHAPTER 8—FRIENDS AND FAMILY

Over the years, I've had friends and family that participated with me drinking, to friends and family in support of this sobriety journey—starting back in high school. I was a jock. I played sports, baseball, basketball, and football, so there was either a party or a kickback every weekend. You had some people who drank, some who smoked weed. I happened to be both. Don't ask me how we were able to get our hands-on alcohol and marijuana.

There wasn't anybody that I can really recall or remember that was like, hey Kenny, you shouldn't drink like that. I remember one time we were pre-gaming at a friend's house, that used to be the kick-in-it spot, no matter where we started or ended the night, it went down there. I was clearly too drunk to get behind the wheel, which was a good thing because it wasn't too often and too many times that I would pass my keys off to a friend and say, hey, can you drive my car?

And I'm really glad and grateful for it because I was extremely drunk that night. Between the ages of like sixteen to about twenty, I drank like crazy. I think it also has to do with location. Because I lived in San Diego, that first couple of years of my adulthood, it was like, okay, we knew where to party, we knew where to hang out, we knew where to meet up to get the alcohol. So, there were a few people, like I said, who didn't drink, and there were a few people who would talk about us, you know, all you guys are alcoholics, you guys are drunk. But we didn't care. We were young and dumb and didn't really understand the ramifications and what can happen later on down the line.

But of course, I probably was the main culprit that experienced it the most, which I was okay with. When I lived in San Diego, I partied in Tijuana, Mexico, like it was no tomorrow, just like anybody else. This was when the border was open, and you didn't have to have a passport when you came back to the states. We would round up however much money we can get and as long as it was $20 to $30 in our pocket, enough money to get us in the club. And most of the clubs were all you can drink. As long as you tip the bartender well, they made sure that you kept coming back to drink, and I was one of them. Luckily, I think once or twice I actually would not necessarily drive into Tijuana, but we would park right at the outlets and things of that nature.

Let me tell you, looking back on it now, hindsight is definitely twenty-twenty, because the drug war and the cartels were just as bad in the late 90s as it probably is today. I lived in a border city, but when I moved to Minnesota, that was a whole different ball game. This was in 2000. I didn't necessarily drink heavily because for one I wasn't familiar with the surroundings, so it was like, hell, I didn't want to be drunk because I can get lost. This was before GPS.

So, if you get lost, you get lost, unless you stopped at a gas station and say, "Hey, where is this location?" So, I was more cautious than ever in my life. I would probably say like the first couple of years, like when I was twenty, twenty-one, no more than twenty-two, and then even when I got up to college at St. Cloud State, we drank. But it was more like, alright, if it's a Wednesday, yeah we might drink. If it's a Thursday, we might drink. Friday, we might drink. Saturday, we might drink. St. Cloud is a small town, probably like the size of National City in terms of population. And so like, there wasn't really like establishments that people of color can really enjoy themselves and hear good music without experiencing racism. And so, you had to be on your guard. You had to be prepared for something to go on because that was just the norm in St. Cloud.

We really didn't think we would get drunk, but it would be like, all right, I have my own apartment. I go to my place. My buddy Kahar lived in the next building in my apartment complex; I might go over to his place or just be outside, talking all night and having drinks. Just like any other college student, I made piss poor, bad decisions. I shouldn't have been around this woman or that woman and talk to this woman or that woman. When you're controlling alcohol and you're allowing alcohol to control your mind, you make bad decisions.

We were all young, so it was like nobody really knew people who were drinking every day, but I wasn't one. I was more like, I got to go to school; usually it was Monday through Wednesday or Monday through Thursday or Tuesdays and Thursdays. Sometimes I have Monday, Wednesday and Friday classes, but for the most part, it was never a time where like, man, I'm so hungover from partying during the week that I couldn't make it to class. And for the most part, like I said, friends and family looked out for us. And you see, the reason why I wanted to talk about this chapter, is that my family did not really, during those early years, may have had ideas that I drank, but I never displayed being drunk and intoxicated.

I can remember that was, but that was maybe like started to get to like maybe when I was like twenty-six or something like that, but not necessarily like right away. It was never a time, like, I don't even recall having those conversations with my family or matter of fact when I turned twenty-one, I didn't even have alcohol in the house. That's just how much respect I had. And if I did, I honestly don't think I really ever drink unless it was like a gathering, like, you know, somebody's birthday or like when I graduated with my bachelor's in, obviously, I drank because I was twenty-three going on twenty-four, so it was okay.

I had a lot of friends, especially those I kept in contact with after I left San Diego. And so, I would call them and discuss the fact my life has been wild. Doing stuff that I wasn't supposed to, multiple women, nights of partying. Despite having conversations with them, I don't necessarily think they knew I had a problem, until I would say like, 2005. When I went to Arizona, my mom never had to say, "Hey, Junior, you need to stop drinking." That happened a couple of times in 2006. It was only a few times that there were issues, but I think like after, after she left, I think that's when the problem started to persist. And like I said, it was a lot of depression. It was a lot of anxiety. It was a lot of disappointment within myself. So, a lot of times, I held a grudge. I kept a lot of frustration inside because I was just like, I worked, I went to so many colleges to get my bachelor's degree. I had hopes in lieu that I would have a job that's paying me some decent money.

And like I said, it hasn't been, or even to this day, like careers paying me good money to where I could be like, okay, I'm over 60- or 70- or 80-grand or something like that. That's what I mean. But I did have a lot of friends that once those problems started to arise, it was like, it would turn into like a regular conversation and then it turned into like drunk dialing. And so, I think that went on for roughly I would say about ten years, so, '05 to '15. It was just like I was on a downward spiral. You know, a lot of my friends couldn't, I guess, I don't think they really understood what issues I was dealing with. Or maybe they just didn't want to tell me if they had issues as far as drinking.

So, I don't know. It's kind of was one of those like confusing things and things like that. But as I mentioned before, I've had a good group of friends that I've been friends with since I was in junior high school, some from elementary, some from high school, and a lot of them have been very supportive. My Brother Zarak Smith barely told me this; he was like, man, you know what I used to do? I used to call him, and he still lives in California to this day. I would call him; it could be anywhere between two hours, three-hour time difference, or even an hour. But a lot of times, he was like, you used to call me all the time and every time you would call, I would just put the phone down and just let you speak. And then the crazy part about it is I've never even known because I was so drunk. And all I was doing was just talking and talking and talking and talking. And because it was so much stuff that was going on in my life, all these failed relationships, all these hurt emotions I had endured that I just couldn't figure out why?

I guess I just couldn't wrap my fingers around it. I could not, because it just seemed concurrent. It just seemed like, I'm in a new relationship, but dang, I got issues, and you know, next relationship. Dang, I got issues. But my friends were there, and I truly appreciate the friends who were there for me before I had this drinking problem. And I appreciate the friends that were there for me during the drinking problem, and I now appreciate those same friends that are the true and not just social media friends. I'm talking about those real true down friends who are still like, man, I got you, man. I'm proud of you, may God be with you, you're doing your thing and overcoming odds. And then the thing about it is that I did not know how much of an impact I would have on people, let alone my friends, let alone my family that now see and understand like, wow, okay, this is who he is. That person that was drinking was a person that was in a very dark place, and that dark place was pain, and a lot of people really and truly couldn't understand it. I'll give you a prime example, and I'll use her name. Her name is Natalie. Not too many people are going to know, but I've been trying my best not to use people's names because it's not to put them down, but it's a fact of opening eyes of just how people can say that they're your friends but will shit on you. Like it is not nothing.

So, this person, Natalie, I knew from 2003, and I'm not going to lie. She was one of those friends that were there for me before I had the drinking problem. She was somewhat there for me when I began to kind of on that downward spiral. But one thing about her is, and I'm not going to make it a race thing. But I don't know if it was just her arrogance as a person or if it was just how she was. But this was 2017, I would say like February or March. Mind you, I just got out of treatment and a couple of months sober.

So, she invites me to a function, and usually, her functions consist of having alcohol there. She had a game night, and I'm not saying that they don't have sober game nights 'cause I'm totally sure that they do. But the crazy part about it is that I asked her straight up, I was like, is it going to be alcohol? She was like, yeah. And then I was like, no, I'm not coming for one. Her townhouse or condo or whatever the hell you want to call her place was too small, and I was not going to be the only sober person in here while I just smelled nothing but alcohol, and then I fuck around and relapse. So, when I told her, hey, I'm not coming. She was just like, you think you're better than everybody, this and this and that. And it wasn't about that. It was about the fact that, hell no, I don't want to go if there's going to be nothing but people drinking alcohol, and these bottles of liquor are still there, setting me up for failure. And needless to say, we haven't been friends since, so that should tell you how much I don't give a fuck. I would cut your ass off if my sobriety is in jeopardy, you know what I mean?

And here's two more stories of two more people, people that I knew: one person I knew since seventh grade, the other person I knew, I believe it was eighth grade, I think it was either eighth or ninth grade; I can't remember. But we all went to school together. And it was all off of a social media post. And I had something that happened to me. Like I said, it was a drinking experience. I think I was seventeen, no, I was sixteen. And we had a party up in the mountains of San Diego. These fuckers, and I'll say it again, these fuckers that I went to high school with, and I'm not going to lie, were primarily the white boys and the Mexicans. And then, like I said, I am not racist. Definitely it's not that.

The reason why I'm saying it is that they had people pay all this money for unlimited drinks, but then they started hiding alcohol. So, of course, you know, young, we find the stash. So instead of drinking the cheap, no-name stuff that they wanted us to drink, we drank up all the expensive stuff. And they ended up tying a buddy of mine to a tree. And that's why I referenced them racist because you tying a black man up to a tree, what does that look like? So, a buddy of mine, JP, tags me and was like, don't you remember this and this and that from that camping trip? And I was like, yeah, I remember it.

So, I asked my homegirl, I was like, so you tell me that you will let your son go on a camping trip and get tied up like black folks did back in the day, you would be okay with that? And so instead of her contacting me and the two of us talk, now mind you, this is still 2017. Like I said, in my first year of sobriety instead of her calling, her best friend reached out. And so, she's talking shit, and I'm like, hold on. First off, this is not got anything to do with you. And you know, she made some references like, oh, you think you just shit because you're sober? I'm like, no, I don't think I'm better than anybody. I'm saying that I made a choice not to drink and can't nobody take away from that.

And so that was the whole thing. So, with that disagreement, I lost two friends, and the only reason I brought those two people up is that they knew my situation as far as my drinking early stages, teenage years, they knew my drinking issues in my twenties. They knew my drinking issues in my thirties. They knew all my relationship problems and issues and all that, but they took it to the extreme. And being that, you know, this, the first person that I knew from seventh grade that she never contacted me, I was like, fuck this. So, I'm deleting, delete, delete, delete. Suddenly, I think it was either earlier this year, 2019, if not sometime in 2018, my friend from seventh grade, she gone sit here and add me on social media, but I'm like, okay, I'm not adding you too, shit. You need to talk to me and get this shit over with. Because like I said, you involved other people when it was just a simple question, but she made it seem like I'm talking about her son, but that wasn't the case. So that didn't go well, but I mean, that's what happens in life. You get older, you know, these same friends you thought were cool, may not be around you for the rest of your life.

As far as family members, there were so many times classes that I had with my father, you know, because he was an alcoholic and now, he sees the same antics that she was doing, but now I'm doing it, you know what I mean? And see, the only difference is that my father, you know, my grandfather passed away in the early '80s. So in a lot of ways, at least from what I know, he didn't see what my dad did after the fact and all of the things that he did and all the stuff that I saw my father when he was under the influence. So, in a lot of ways I don't think my father really knew how to handle it. So that's why we've butted heads. We butted heads basically since I was fifteen into the current day. It's a fucking shame. But like I said, that's just how it is. And I'm sorry to say, but in a lot of ways I do feel like, my father can throw in my face how much money he has. He's done it numerous times, but I think the jealousy comes in as far as my father because the life that I've lived is not remotely close and comparable to what he did.

And as far as being able to go to school, go to the military and still right now to this day make more money than him or get out on disability and I make more than him. I'm not talking about his postal retirement. I'm talking about my disability through the VA, and like I said, I don't have to work. He retired two times from two careers. And so, it's like I am not mad. I am not hating. That's my father, and I love him. But like I said, I don't think he's truly understood like what it is exactly I've been through, and I'm not mad at it. I'm not the least bit mad, but at the same token, I want to be respected for what I've done.

I want to be respected for each accomplishment I've had in my life. There are reasons why, and I'm thankful, and I'm going to say this over and over. I'm thankful for my friends. I'm thankful for my family members. I'm thankful for the co-workers that I've met along the way that may have seen at this job or saw me as being quiet and never thought that I would be that person that would have any kind of issues with drinking and I will say this to close this chapter out; I did have supporters as far as my family.

My mother, she just wanted to see me happy. She wanted to see me sober. She wanted to see me not in this predicament anymore. And like I said to her right now, all the stuff that I'm doing, I'm sure it's just a surprise, but it's a good feeling to know that, okay, her son took care of business; got his shit together. You know, the same thing with my sister Laquisha, she has been a supporter. She's seen me and knows those episodes of drinking in my twenties. And it's good to have those people, you know, my brother Anthony the same way. He's put up with a lot of stuff that I've done. My brother Michael is the same way. And some of my best friends, Shawn, Anthony,

Freddie, Kahar, and Washington, and a host of amazing people that I've met along this journey.

All my Grandma, Sally (Dea') Watson wanted, was to see me sober. She actually got the chance to see that in person and on video chat. My Grandma passed away in February 2020. My world stopped, and I was numb. The first thing that came to mind was when I surprised her for her birthday 2017. We sat and talked like we did when I was a kid. I felt prideful, a Watson sober, a master's degree, and a lifetime ahead of me to keep the legacy going. The next day my father asked me not to attend the funeral because of some past family drama. I intended to go to the funeral to pay my respects and go home. I wanted to drink that day. My buddy Kettler from church came over and we fellowshipped, I got my tears out and gave it to God. Dea' came to me in a dream days later, and she told me, I am the chosen one, she loved me, and to keep going on this path. I LOVE U Dea'. RIP.

CHAPTER 9—SOBER FACES

I'm a month into my graduate program at St. Cloud State, so around March of 2017, I was on my way to South Africa to a study abroad at Nelson Mandela University. I was very nervous that I was going to be on a plane pretty much twenty-four hours. But the heaviest thing on my mind was the reaction that my soon to be ex-wife would react to getting served the papers for the divorce. So, I went ahead, happy, you know, arrived at the hotel, and checked my email. And there it was! An email from my attorney. So, of course, I'm nervous and wasn't sure if I really wanted to open the email. I opened it, and she said that she was served, and gave the detail of what she was wearing and things like that. I guess I was happy yet fearful, not knowing that she was going to actually come to Minnesota. And so, I had to wait. But hey, I got to celebrate in South Africa.

So, I thought that was pretty dope. It was a free trip under my Post 911, GI Bill. So, shout out to the government, Veteran's Administration, for paying for the entire trip! So, I'm very thankful for that life-changing experience. Very, very, very, thankful. Man, I got to study abroad in South Africa! A dream of mine since I was a kid.

Nelson Mandela University was a campus was like no other. The views in the background made for any picture you hang on the wall. The most amazing thing about my trip was how the people were so humble. We went to this one area; it was, I would say, like, their version of the projects. And the worst, definitely worst, from the moment I stepped off the bus and started, like, meeting the kids, meeting some of the elders in the community. It felt like home; the people looked like me. The bone structure, just like my mom in the face. And I was just like, "This is crazy," I felt like I knew where I came from. It was pretty dope too, that a little kid had on the San Diego T-shirt. You know I had to take a picture with that little kid. Shout out to San Diego.

On the trip I had, I don't know if you want to call it an epiphany. But it definitely was something that gave me a great feeling with the path I was headed on. I kept to myself on some parts of the trip because I didn't want to be around the students who were drinking. So, the best thing is to keep for myself, but I had a lot of free time in South Africa. I'm not going to lie. This is like my first two or three months of grad school.

I come back to Minnesota after the two-week trip. Now it was a waiting game to hear back from the courts. A few weeks went by, and I finally got the notification. It said that I had so many days to respond, and I think it was thirty days from the date she received the divorce papers. Nichele sent harassing text messages while I was in treatment about getting a divorce and now refusing to respond.

So, we had to send her another one, and there still was no response. By this time, it was April, and I got a letter saying I had to go to court. This was the day I had to go in for the divorce proceeding. So, I was extremely nervous, just for the simple fact of like, what if she tries to come through the door and asks a judge for me to give her money and this and that. If that hadn't happened, I would have been able to get money from her because I'm on disability. So, it actually would have backfired if she were to show up. So, they went ahead, the judge gave her an hour and a half to show, and she didn't show up. The judge decided to go ahead and proceed.

The judge had me take a seat. I was sworn in. It felt like I got in trouble or was on trial. The judge was polite, but it's just certain places that you don't want to be. The judge asked me some questions, and I answered. My attorney was sitting at the other table and cross-examined me. I don't know if that was how it was supposed to have been if she would have come with an attorney and probably would have been sitting together.

She asked me questions, and like, it just seemed like I couldn't speak clearly because then at that point, it was like the pain that I suffered throughout the marriage was coming out with those words. And it just kind of was like in that little bit of time of being in that court, I think I was in that court for almost two hours. Good and bad things played through my mind. And I was just like, wow, how am I still alive? Like, I don't understand. And that's the part that's like, so crazy. And hopefully, you know, I'm at a different point in my life, so I'm not as upset. Not to sound greedy, but I wish I would have asked for money because I knew I was entitled to it. I knew that it was done, and I haven't looked back.

So, I drove back to St. Cloud, and one of my grad school classmates called me to check on how the court went. He came and picked me up and went over to his place. I was over there for at least four, maybe five hours, and we left around like eleven. I felt like these are some real dudes. I laughed and didn't think about the divorce. I didn't think about anything. I was just more or less only in the moment. I got to know his brother and his cousin, and I thought that was pretty dope. Sometimes when you meet new people, not everybody's going to get along, but it was like the moment I walked in, that we talked trash.

I got involved with this community outreach program, building leadership in the city of St. Cloud. It was the Juggad Leadership Program. I learned a lot. I met people, some movers and shakers in the city.

So, I was chatting online with a woman from high school. She eventually moved out a month or so later. It was toward the end of my first semester and like maybe a week or about a week or two before the end of the semester, and she helped me with my final assignments. So, I got done or whatever, like the semester she went with me to my nephew Marcel's graduation, met my family brothers, stuff like that, but it just didn't feel genuine to me. Despite all of that, for the majority of the time she lived with me, she wasn't working. She felt like she was running the place. I had to let her know that it was my place, the only person on the lease. And that nobody will come into my place and tell me what to do. So she had to go.

It was like a real smooth transition. I DJ'd St. Cloud's Juneteenth celebration. Dijon was in the Jugaad Leadership Program as well. I just wanted a friend, somebody to hang out with because I was missing female companionship, not necessarily sex. We dated probably I would say little over three months. June until September. She helped me out financially, and sometimes he bought me food groceries, and stuff and I appreciated the good deed. My car broke down, and she paid for my car to be fixed. When I got money, I gave it back to her. Maybe she thought I was lying when I said I was going to pay her back.

I got my financial aid check I was getting ready to go to Mississippi, and she begged for $500 plus $500 I already owed her. I knew I was going to get the money back. I knew that I wasn't going to see it, or whatever. She was rushing marriage. She wanted to be married like the following year. Basically, that didn't last; I had a falling out with the Mayor's assistant because he made an inappropriate comment. She took his side when I had to let it be known that I would have to have a conversation with him. She started calling me crazy. The deal breaker was how disrespectful her daughter was. I just dealt with disrespectful ass kids in a marriage and wasn't having it go on again. I'm in a better place. I'm happy now but the struggles of that and then having to maintain going to grad school. In fact, I almost quit because of the relationship with her. But luckily, I talked to Kahar. And he told me life is going to be all right. Hang in there. Just do the work, go to class, and I took it to heart.

I appreciate that, Kahar. We've been hanging tough since 2001. But I went ahead, and I finished the semester, you know, I did okay. I could have done better, but a lot of times I just didn't really understand how to write correctly, and that's what I struggled with. I should have gone to writing lab probably like every other day or something because I know that I can be expressive, but it's hard to put it on paper and not say it in a way that I'm speaking.

This journey has been tough. The journeys have been brutal. The journey has probably seen me cry more than perhaps ever have, but I feel better. I wasn't really messing with anybody. Kind of went with the flow and focused on finishing my master's program. I did some traveling. I went to San Diego during spring break of 2018. I stayed at one of the oldest hotels downtown. Every time I go back to San Diego, everything seems so much smaller. I grew up right here, and I have many memories. I had to get a shrimp burrito from Lolita's and walked next door and got a Slurpee from 7-Eleven. Another sober trip in the books. Let's see where the train ends up.

I went to DC a few months later with my second fiancé Patrice. It was really cool to visit. Seeing that the last time I was here, I was forced by the Army to go to treatment. I got the chance to go to Arlington, Virginia, and went to this loading dock. The same loading dock I went to before entering treatment in 2014. So that was pretty cool to go back and just reflect what has happened in my life that last four years. I also had the chance to visit the African-American history museum. I returned from that trip, knowing I had one class to finish in my program, and I would have a master's degree in hand. I made a promise to myself that I would pursue dating in January 2019. Let's just say my mind changed on my trip to Ohio.

CHAPTER 10—WHITNEY

With all the health issues I racked up from drinking, I have been trying my best to change my eating habits. It hasn't been easy. But I know that is something that I needed to take advantage of. One of my sister's friends from high school suggested various social media groups that were vegetarian or vegan-based, and they were also geared towards African Americans. I joined multiple groups, not necessarily thinking that this potentially can be helpful as far as prepping to make meals. I didn't really participate, didn't comment on people's pages or posts. I would just look and see what vegan meals look like and would it necessarily be edible to me. And I remember it was October, the weekend of October the 13th or something like that. I happened to be in Cleveland, Ohio, in town for the LA Chargers game against the Cleveland Browns. My dad and I met up and everything.

I was scrolling through Facebook, and one of the vegan groups said, "Alright fella's, we want to see what you look like in suits, so post a picture." Over the last two years, I had been wearing different suits to various community events in St. Cloud and wanted to see what others thought of how I looked in them. I didn't think that I would get a response the way that I did. Mind you, I'm in Cleveland doing something totally different, doing a bonding experience with my dad, and going to a football game—something I never did as a child. The response from women was pretty quick. I wish I could find that post and texts to see what was the final number of likes. But I started to see more and more and more likes. In my mind, I was thinking I might be able to find a companion.

I looked at a few profiles. There was one woman that eventually I found out that was actually in her fifties, but she was very beautiful, and I would have thought that she was potentially like thirty-five. She looked twenty years younger. And, I told her straight up, I was like, hello, I'm thirty-nine and I don't have any kids. She told me she had full-grown kids, got grandkids, and told me I was too young. So, I was like, all right, you know, no harm, no foul. And I kept it moving.

And so, I think I messaged like one other person, and I truly can't recall if she responded, but there was another profile that I had gone on. I looked at the profile and thought to myself, she's got to be taken. The only way you are going to find out is to leave a message. So, I went ahead and left a message, and she responded, give or take thirty minutes. She responded. No kids, didn't drink, didn't smoke, didn't party, all the things that, in the back of the mind, this is too good to be true. This can't be a real person. And now mind you, she was very beautiful, she was a very, very, very beautiful person, good heart, just good everything. I was honest with her. I told her, "I'm in Cleveland getting ready to go to this football game. And I would reach out after the game."

The game was cool, but I was intrigued. Whitney was all I could think about. We exchanged messages on Facebook for about two days; it was cool. Then that third day, Whitney asked if I wanted to video chat. "Heck yeah." was my response. We have the first call; her face popped up on my phone, I was like, this is the woman I can see myself marrying. I don't know why. That first conversation was really cool. It was just us going back and forth, we were laughing, there wasn't a dull moment.

This was a conversation with substance. Whitney seemed to have her head screwed on, headed in the right direction. In my mind, I was telling myself this might work. Do I want to give it a chance? I was in a sexual relationship with a much younger woman when Whitney and I met. She knows this because I told her that upfront. That's why I was like, I'd rather talk to this woman I've met online who lives in Florida, than to continue the relationship with this woman who lived in the same city as me. After that first initial video chat, we talked every day, and it just seemed like, wow, this is natural. I can be myself, but I'm just not in the same state or city as her. I was ready to meet Whitney in person.

As a gift to myself and completion of grad school, I now wanted to return to my birthplace. It was truly a blessing to find out Whitney was from Jacksonville, born and raised. Felt like the stars were aligned, which may be the right time and the right situation for me because I told myself, I would date in 2019. I had relationships early in sobriety and they were all disastrous.

And so, I didn't feel the need at that particular moment to be in a relationship. So, after 2017, I just didn't get involved with anybody. I was 100% single all of 2018, which was very strange. Not strange, but it was just like, I thought something was wrong with me, but it wasn't. It was time for me to focus on my health, my sobriety, and the idea of relying on another woman. The long-distance relationship that we had, it was companionship. It was cool. And the good thing about it is that, I guess she thought I was joking when I was like, yeah, I want to come out there to visit.

So, I waited until a couple of days after Christmas and flew out to Jacksonville. I was out there for roughly about six days, and there were a lot of things that we did that was different. I got to see the sunrise New Year's Day 2019 at Jacksonville Beach. I've never done that, but I've always wanted to. We went to her church a couple of times. It was cool because I did say that I wanted the person that I'm with to be active in the church. Even though I'm not the most active as I should be in church, but I was like, maybe she can turn me around and stuff.

Overall, it was a good trip and, it made me want to come back. The good thing about it is that I respected her; what I mean by that is the physical. I mean, I've been in situations where I'm a sexual beast, and it wasn't about that. It was more or less like, let me make love to your mind, let me get all those orgasmic thoughts over the physical, and trust me she was worth it and still is. One thing I like about my situation with Whitney, she really took my sobriety to heart. Our first date was at a speakeasy. We didn't stay long because it was tiny and they had us sitting at the bar.

The good thing about it is that we talked about her coming to visit me for Valentine's Day weekend because my brother had turned fifty earlier this year. I'm, okay, well this is a perfect opportunity for us to celebrate Valentine's Day, and meet my family when we celebrate my brother's birthday. This was amazing. What I liked about it was that Whitney fit right in. It wasn't like this was her first time being around my family. That's one thing I think is by far the sexiest thing or quality a woman can have is how you can fit in with that person's family. And trust me, she did. It was cool, and I wished that I could have shown her around Minnesota a different time of the year, obviously, because there was snow on the ground and it was cold; so there wasn't much we could do.

My best friend Shawn was in town too. So it was like I was entertaining two people, but it was good for him to come out. So that's why I wasn't really tripping. But yeah, I think that everything that has happened thus far has been amazing and then to show that I meant business. I came back. I think it was a couple of days after her birthday in March. And I thought it was cool because it was like we're making an effort to do things and be around each other. I think it was between the December and January trips that gave me a push in the direction of wanting to be in a relationship and wanting to relocate to Florida.

But I was uncertain I could do it, not sure if I had the funds, plus I was just adjusting to living back in Minnesota. I wasn't feeling Minnesota winters; it was just the fact that my family is here. I could get in a car, drive an hour, and I can chill with my nephew. I could chill with my mom; I could chill with my sister, my niece and nephews, or whomever if they're not busy including my brother-in-law. But I still didn't really have any friends, and sometimes it was difficult, sometimes it was hard. But yeah, so I went ahead. I think after that March trip, I was already in the mode of let's go ahead and plan this move and let me tell you it wasn't easy.

And even being here, currently going on month five, is still not the easiest thing, but I know that it has been well worth it, well worth making that decision to come to Florida. The next couple of months was difficult because all my funds had to go towards the move to Florida. Not going to lie to you, there were so many times in my mind that I didn't think that I was going to make it out to Jacksonville only because money was really funny. But I thank God that everything worked itself out.

It's one thing to deal with somebody on a long distance and then to get in the same city and state with that person and then you're seeing that person on a more consistent basis, obviously not, five days and then I won't see you again for two months or something like that. I just communicated that with my lady just the other day, the idea of just not being used to somebody being nice, somebody like really caring about me. And because for the last, honestly, like the last nine years, I can't say nine I would say the last eight years, it hasn't been that way where somebody truly cared about me and a needless to say. In those nine years, I only had one serious relationship, and that was my marriage, and I wasn't appreciated. I wasn't looked out for or anything. It was like I'm doing for her, but she is not doing it for me. So for me to be in this completely new relationship, new city, and state, I had to get used to my lady being so kind and sincere with me because I was so used to women being basically vultures and leeches, trying to suck me dry as far as my money—these are all facts—these are not lies. These are the truth. And you know, we've done a lot since I've been here; we've been to Orlando two times. We've done stuff around the city of Jacksonville: farmers' markets, various organic supermarkets, mom and pop corner stores, and produce stores.

The one thing I can say about my relationship now than what it was last year it's different because we're physical with each other over not being together. So, it's been difficult. But then it's also been really good to have that companionship on a consistent basis because I've been so used not to having it. As I said, the good thing about it is that my lady, she's thirty-one, no kids, master's degree, and a physiotherapist. So, it's like if I really have those problems, I can honestly go to my lady and she'll listen if I have to vent and so on. I also wanted to acknowledge her family, her stepmom, her dad, and I've only really gotten to know one of her three sisters. They're all nice and respectful.

It was hit and miss. It's like you got some that I'm still cool with to this day. And then you got those who sided with their family member even though their family member was a piece of shit because that's what my ex-wife was, and still is. So, it's just a lot of getting used to. And of course, a woman's going to lie, and the family's going to believe her despite the fact that what I've achieved in the last three and a half years, was away from my ex-wife.

I have different feelings about my relationship with

Whitney. It's why we go for counselling. I really love Whitney. She's everything that I have envisioned in a woman, and probably the last nineteen years is just now it's finally coming to fruition, to reality, and I'm thankful. I thank God as much as I can. I know that I'm not going to sit here and say that our relationship has been picture perfect because it hasn't, but just the idea that I'm in a real relationship, something that I haven't had in quite some time and it's a learning experience.

We have tough days, good days, but those good days outweighed any tough days we have had thus far. We're both entrepreneurs. It's just a matter of us pushing each other to get to that next level. And I foresee that happening. The good thing about it is that we're going to go to two different counsellors to make sure. We're going to couples counselling with the VA and with the Pastor and his wife at Whitney's church. So that's the good thing we're trying avenues to make sure that this is the right thing and how this can work.

And I believe in my heart that it will because we're still here. We didn't give up; we didn't walk away. I look forward to the growth and the potential that we both have. And to be eventually at that point where we are truly 100% working for ourselves and not working for anybody else, but still, make enough money to survive, travel, have fun and make road trips, have additions to the family, and so forth. I look forward to making great memories with you, my "Sweets." Stay tuned to the *Me and Sweets* book and YouTube page coming real soon.

CHAPTER 11—MENTAL HEALTH

Growing up watching my father dealing with alcoholism, infidelity, and all-around not being there for me, had a lot to do with some of my mental health issues. Being counted out by various school administrators in schools and I like to say hello to those counsellors, and they're probably retired by now. Still, those counsellors said that I probably wouldn't even go to a junior college, but here I am, PhD level. It's kind of crazy, isn't it. Twenty-two or twenty-three years ago, somebody told me that I probably wouldn't even make it at a junior in college. So, it goes to show, you know what I mean? And that's what happened. A lot of people told me I couldn't do this.

When I played sports, they told me I wasn't good enough. They said I can't play football despite being one of the best players out there. They didn't give a fuck about that. They wanted to play the white boys and Mexicans, not a racist statement, just stating the truth. I experienced a lot of things. I can remember the first time somebody told me that they were pregnant. I was fourteen, embarrassed by that situation. And that stuck with me for a long time, and I was just thinking about this the other day that if I hadn't taken a paternity test at fifteen, I would have a twenty-five-year-old daughter right now, believe it or not. So, I thank my mom for that, because she was there, she took me to the County of San Diego to take a paternity test. I found out on my sixteenth birthday. I wasn’t the father after being harassed for over a year and a half.

I was seventeen dating the girl at my high school. She told me she was pregnant three or four different times, and I won't mention her name, but I really wondered to this day, was she ever pregnant? Or were you pregnant by somebody else, but you knew that I was just the gullible guy who would believe it? Of course, she never had any miscarriage, supposedly abortion, supposedly, whatever. You know, it's just like, it's so much stuff. It's so much to the point where it's like, I really, and truly I didn't even look in a mirror. There were a lot of times where I would just brush my teeth. I would never really look myself in the eye because I was afraid.

I was so afraid of who's going to find out. I was so afraid of the friendships that I would lose. I was so ashamed of family members, you know, disliking me or whatever, or hiding the alcohol because that was the case. But I had some serious issues, and the thing about it is, the military is when I started getting in trouble for alcohol, I was like, man you got to go talk to somebody. And I did. And despite the fact that me going to talk to somebody was my excuse to get out of work, it felt good to vent. It really and truly felt good just to get whatever was on my mind, on my heart at that moment, or even be able to revisit things that may have occurred in my past growing up.

All these resources were beneficial. I was frequently going to a therapist, and I'm not ashamed to say it. My message to the readers is that this is not just for anybody who has issues with a substance; if you got problems, try your best to seek professional help. Even if they write in the notes that you are one of the craziest motherfuckers, at least you got it off your chest.

Moving back to Jacksonville forty years later, I found myself facing new challenges ahead: not knowing people, finding my way around a new city, adjusting to this heat. I love seafood, so no complaints there. I was away from my family that held me accountable in Minnesota. In an African-American household, mental health isn't a topic people like to address. They might address that person as that different cousin, uncle, brother. But nobody would necessarily be like, hey, this person has mental health issues. And being that we're going into a new decade, it's very important that you go, even if you go once a month, if you go every six months or whatever it is, we all go through problems that we just can't solve. We may have issues at work; we may have issues with our relationships. We may have issues dealing with reality because, I'm a tell you, one of the many reasons why I have chosen not to go back to work is because I can't deal with people. I don't have that patience that I once had. The military is to blame for that, and the person now in the leadership role who was above me, failed me.

In 2020 as far as goals and aspirations, I want to continue writing books. I have a few more books in the works. I really want to launch my DJ business here in Jacksonville. I want to do public speaking. This book will allow me the platform to speak my truths in hopes of helping others out there still struggling with personal issues. The "negative me" is no longer. That person that struggled with substance abuse is no longer, and now this person has all these aspirations because you can set those goals and now be able to achieve them compared to before. I'm going to stop drinking. But then I said that over and over, over and over. But when I was saying I will change, it was the opposite. It was like, shut up, I will change, but not right now, I'm going to go ahead and take this drink. I will drink as much as I can at night. I wake up tomorrow, sick as a dog, hungover, stomachache, throwing up, diarrhea, all that, and I'm a change.

I see people who post off on social media. I won't call anybody out, but I see it all the time. Every single weekend, Fridays, Saturday nights, somebody saying or Sunday morning or Monday morning, "Oh I'm never drinking again." I was that person, and so what I do just to poke fun at them, “Hey you better drink you some water, it'll help you.”

So, like I said, if you have any questions, you have any testimonies you want to share, you can reach me on my social media, personal email, YouTube, Facebook, Instagram or Twitter. I'm human, I've made a lot of mistakes. I've hurt a lot of people, but I don't want to do it anymore. I want to enjoy the rest of my life. Sober, free, and clear of alcohol. So, I thank-you, guys. I appreciate the fact that you've been able to get a little bit of a taste of my life, my struggles with alcohol, and a few added bonuses.

CHAPTER 12—CONCLUDING REMARKS

Thank God it's finally over. I guess you can say I've been putting off this last chapter for various reasons. I want to start with current events and then kind of work my way back. This past Sunday, December 8, I got a chance to, I guess you can say a tradition that I started back in 2017, go to various National Football League (NFL) games. The first year was in Minnesota, Minnesota Vikings against the Los Angeles Rams. I believe the Los Angeles Rams won that game. Last year I went to a game in Cleveland, Ohio. The Los Angeles Chargers played against the Cleveland Browns; the Chargers won. And just this past Saturday, I went to see Jacksonville Jaguars versus the LA Chargers game. It was cool, and I mean that literally, but not really, it was just overcast.

But I got a chance to do what I did last year, went a couple of hours before kick-off. Got a chance to, you know, view the stadium before it got packed, and got a chance to see some of the Chargers as they were warming up. I thought that was pretty cool. That was, I guess you can say, a delayed fortieth birthday gift, a delayed three-year sober anniversary gift to myself because I felt like I deserved it. This is something that I have started, and I'm going to start trying to do this like every year. I've already got one buddy on board from St. Cloud State, my buddy Joe Titus. He said, you know, wherever I choose as far as the game to go to, he'll try to come out, which I thought was pretty dope. And then like I said, you know, with each year I can add somebody else to come with me on the journey.

Have a good time; get good seats—just fellowship. And the good thing about it is the people who I went to this game with were my lady's dad, well my girlfriend's dad and my girlfriend's sister's boyfriend. The three of us went, you know, it was kind of like a, just a Sunday fun day for us men. And it was cool. You see, I enjoy it myself, a lot of laughs, a lot of cheers, louder interacting with just fans in general, Jaguar fans, Charger fans, and actually bumped into somebody that I went to high school with. I didn't know him, but we were going to high school together at Helix High School in LA Mesa, California. So I thought that was pretty unique.

You know, this is how I am now. I like to travel. I like to go to different sporting arenas or stadiums and watch games. Even though, you get a chance every Sunday or Thursday or Monday to watch NFL football or even college games on Fridays and Saturdays, you're still sitting here watching this on a television set compared to seeing it live in person. It's two totally different experiences. So, and like I said, these are the type of activities that I enjoy doing sober. If I would've been going to these events before getting sober, I'd probably be drunk off my behind just like any and everybody else. I am not going to say everybody in the arena, or stadium, but you get what I'm saying. *12 Faces of Sober* has been a journey: being able to verbalize, to get this off of my chest. My truths in terms of my journey prior to sobriety are those twelve years of battling the addiction of alcohol and the twelve years of failed relationships.

I was dealing with some bad people and dealing with some good people during those twelve years. Gaining friends, losing friends, regaining friends, you know, relationships with family members lost. But this is my life. These are my decisions. These are my choices. These are the people that I want to deal with. These are the people that I want to have in my life. Can't nobody tell me at this point, I'm forty years old. So, whether or not people like my decisions, guess what? You don't have to talk to me. And you know, I did something that I didn't think that I wanted to do. I'm going to share this because this goes to show how people can be, you know, I was in the situation, we won't name the person's name, and I won't name the time, but I was dealing with somebody, and their car got towed; that person had no money.

You know, it was towards the end of the month for me. Of course, I didn't have any money, so I got a loan from Pops to get this person's car out of towing, and sure enough, got it done. And that individual and I had a falling out. And you know, I just cut it short, and I said, you know, I'm going to try something out just to see what this person is going to say. So, I shot her a text, you know, what's up with this money, you know, this person had all the negative things to say to me. First she tried to say, oh, that I'm faking PTSD despite being clinically diagnosed with it, by doctors from the Army and from the VA in two different States. So, to that one person, she's out there, I don't know where she is.

But, the joke's on you because I'm no loser. I'm nobody who, you know, is out here in the game that's trying to screw over anybody. I'm to myself, and that's for a reason, I keep to myself because I just personally don't want to, cause a lot of people don't understand this, the journey of sobriety. You know, there's a lot of people out there that their whole mentality is: What can I do to get over on the next person? And she was one of them. And like I said, see what people don't realize is that I'm no longer that person who's going to be a pushover. And I'm sorry to say it like this for a piece of ass.

And guess what, she is not a part of my life and I'm pretty sure she is making no money anyway. You know what I'm saying? Because of her criminal record, and see that's the whole thing, a lot of people want to talk about me, a lot of people want to say something about me, but a lot of people got these, you know, they're lying, they're lying to society, they're lying to their own family, they're lying to their friends. They're lying to the state boards of Arizona saying that they're one thing, but they're not. I'm just a recovering alcoholic who's had stumbles along the way in this thing called life, but you also have to understand, I was counted out by many, but I was able to pick myself up and say, enough is enough. Now let's do something else.

Sure enough, that's what happened. I got sober, and then life is just that much different: the way I think, the way I process things, the way I have relationships with my family, the way I have relationships with my friends, and how I have a relationship with the person that I'm dating. These are all things that I had problems with when I was drinking. Now it's just like, okay, life is not perfect, but it's a lot better than it was when I was drinking. Now, as I stated throughout this book, I struggled with alcohol because I was dealing with bad women. I struggled with alcohol because I wasn't happy in terms of career or lack thereof, the pay scale or military life, family separation, abuse from an ex-spouse, you know, falling outs with family members, people not understanding what and why and how it got to the point of twelve years of alcoholism.

I'm sorry. You know, I can, I will say it once, and I'll

say it this time, I apologize, and I'm sorry from the bottom of my heart for any and everybody that I've ever hurt or ever said something or ever did anything crazy or even embarrassed you. But a lot of people really and truly never asked me like what's really going on. Even to this day, some of the challenges that I've faced is when nobody truly understands why I chose to drink all those years. Nobody truly understands why I gave it up. But I'll give you a few reasons why. Like I said, drinking was just a norm. You know, just have a couple of drinks with friends or family or a person you may be dating, but the abuse came when my money started running low and not getting called back for job interviews or jobs. They were telling me I'm too qualified because I have an education.

And it's like, in the back of my mind, I'm digging like, why did I go to college? You know, why did I do internships? Why did I get out here and try to get my name out to the public. For people to say, no, we can't give you a job or the job is only going to pay you $10 and $11 an hour? This is a fact, but I won't name the companies, as it's almost three years ago. The job offered me $11 an hour and what? I'm forty now, so I was thirty-six or thirty-seven then. So yeah, those are the types of things that I've faced.

You learn, you live, and you learn more. You know, and the primary reason I chose to get sober is that it was hurting my mom, it was hurting my sister, and I just didn't want to go through it anymore.

I really did not want to go through that pain that I saw when they gave me a recap of something that I did while I was drinking. So, the good part about it is that you know, I don't drink anymore. I'm not going to sit here and say I'm the happiest man on the planet because I still battle with a lot of different things. But the good thing about it is that you know, I can wake up and not have that one or have that desire for alcohol like I once did. And it's just crazy that it is three years this upcoming Sunday, December 15, we'll make it three years in one month. And you know, this is a good feeling. This is an awesome, amazing feeling to know that I cannot worry about alcohol and what has taken me so long to finish.

This is because I didn't know what I wanted to put in the conclusion. So, seeing that my conclusion is just like any other chapter in this book, meaning that I could say you do and put anything in it because this is my book. But I wanted to touch on the actual idea of what I've done in a matter of three years. And I know people say, all right, well, *12 Faces of Sober*, was supposed to be the first year of sobriety, but it was just like a lot of things are going on to where I just didn't have the opportunity to really sit down. But guess what, now I can share it. The first year of sobriety was the hardest. The first month of sobriety was even harder. I kept myself busy by traveling. I kept myself busy by volunteering.

Being a part of the community just to keep me away from idle time, and I guess you can say it worked. I didn't think that it was going to work. I had two, possibly three situations of women that I was talking to that was like none of them was going where it needed to be. But by the same token I was like, all right, well almost quit school because of, but then I knew that these relationships were temporary and this degree is permanent. So, of course, I buckled down and finished that first year of school in Virginia, definitely tough. And it's kind of one of those things where when you have your mind set forth on something, anything is possible. Like with my master's degree, I was on like literally one class away from finishing in three semesters. Who would have thought this old dude could have finished in three semesters, but my adviser did it on purpose and held me back, so to speak. But it is what it is. As I mentioned before in a previous chapter, I got a chance to go to San Diego a couple of times. Two times while sober and one time when I was transitioning, about to go into treatment. I've been everywhere, not everywhere, but I've been to places that I wouldn't have been. You know, I came to Jacksonville to visit twice before moving here. I went to Mississippi, New York, Brooklyn, Ohio, Cleveland, Akron.

It's a lot of other places that I definitely went to. Oh, I went to DC as well. I know I mentioned this, and I'm repeating it because I want you guys to know that like these were things that I was limited to doing when I was married. I couldn't just up and say, all right, I want to go here. It was like she wanted to go somewhere and I had to agree to it. If not, she was going by herself. So that's a good thing. I see differences there. I can now make decisions for myself over somebody making them for me. That's the blessings. That's the true blessings that I have, and I promise you I'm not trying to change it, nor am I going to let somebody step into my life and change that for me. Like I said, the relationship, you know, my friends, they believe in me, and they know that if I want to be on some other stuff, then I would, but you know, they know who I am, and they see the guy just more mature.

They see the guy who now doesn't have an alcohol problem and is just older. I've toyed around with different ventures as far as what I want to do, and I guess that's the good thing. You know, I don't have any responsibilities, so that I can make these types of decisions. Most people can't, because by now, you know, you're forty, you're probably married, have three or four kids; three of those kids could be in college, whatever it is. But I haven't had that, so I've been fortunate enough not to have had kids yet. And that time will come. I think that it was more or less that I have had to get my shit together before I can honestly bring another human life into existence. It's coming closer, you never know, 2020, 2021 could be that time for me to be a father finally.

But I'm ready; I'm welcoming it. I mean, I barely sleep now so I could do some magic. I'll probably be up all night just chilling, having conversations with my child, sleep, or not sleep. That's the difference, the luxury of already planning those types of things out. 2020, like I said, it's coming up with what I plan on doing this year. I have a couple of company business ventures that I'm trying, you know. I would love, love, love, love, love, love to have the opportunity to not only use this book as a tool but be able to speak on it, to speak on my experiences. Things that might not even be in this book that I will also have the opportunity to share with you; that's what this is about. We sometimes struggle, and we don't know who to turn to, or when we do turn to somebody, how to say it; now I just say it.

It's no problem, no issues. But for those individuals that they cannot be expressive in terms of their genuine emotions, I want to be able to help them or help you so that you don't have to turn to alcohol and be like, all right, now that I got this liquid courage in my system, now I can tell you how I feel. I tell you, I mean my message to you or to anybody who purchased this book and read it all the way up until this chapter; I want you to understand from the bottom of my heart that this is not for show. This is really how my life was or still is, and nobody came to refute or debate these issues because it's all documented. And if you don't believe me, you can follow me on social media, and you can see it, especially on Facebook, where I actually put, you know, I put stuff into words on top of the pictures.

What were my emotions; what were my feelings? How did I handle this? What did I do in that situation? Guess what? I chose not to do that. I chose to do this freestyle from the heart. No, no cue cards, no nothing, nobody helping me. It's just me and my heart talking and the only thing I could say as far as advice to anybody who does have issues and struggles with alcohol, get help, and get help immediately. Don't wait too long because you don't want hospital visits or hospital stays, rides, and ambulances thinking like, man, this could be the end of your life.

Don't be that person. Don't let your kidneys go. Don't

let your pancreas go. Don't let your liver go or punish your body because you don't know how to communicate or express your feelings. Look, it only took alcohol, I would say eight out of the ten times for me to be expressive and tell it how it was or how I was really feeling, and I think in a lot of ways it came out worse instead of better. But at least I know now I can correct it because if I have a problem, if I have a disagreement, I could just think about it for a little bit and they'd be like, well, you know what? Here it is what you're going to do about it.

I really and truly want to close this chapter out with just this message. Alcohol at one point tasted good, but just because something tastes good to you, does it necessarily mean it's good for you! It can land you in jail, lose your license, get a felony, get a misdemeanor, and lose your job. You can be embarrassed on your job; you could be made an example of that on your job; your mugshot could be presented at the job. These are all things that happened to me. I am not going to say when and how, but it happened, and I'm not prideful, but it was my life. It was my decisions and the choices I made. Nobody held a gun to my head and said, hey Kenny, you got to drink. It was more or less like Kenny, go get you something to drink.

Okay. Like I said, anybody that's looking for guidance, advice, I'm here, I'm open, you know, I will say twenty-four, seven, but sometimes I need to get a little bit of sleep. But like I said, you guys can reach me via social media if you want to talk. You hit me via email. I know for sure that I've posted it or stated it in one of my chapters. And like I said, it will be at the beginning of the book as well if you didn't catch it. I've appreciated every last person that has hit like, left a comment, shared, went to my YouTube page and viewed my videos.

I've appreciated all of that because every time I see that notification saying somebody liked your page, somebody commented on your page, somebody shared your page; it has motivated me to finish this book. It has motivated me to already have in mind the sequel to this book, which will be amazing. So, look forward to *Three Years*, my next book. It won't be spelled out in three or the number three, but it'll be spelled a little bit different. But that's coming soon. You know, I want to thank everybody. I really and sincerely hope that you guys have enjoyed this book. I hope that it's one of those books where you can just not only read it once or reread it. If you're a scholar or professor and you decide you want to share this in the class, hopefully, it can be a book that's used every semester or every school calendar year for, you know, for some time because it's a book that can help.

It's a book that can inspire, I mean, just keep in mind that things that I've had my hands in since being sober, you know, as far as education, I looked, I tried culinary arts, but thanks to the school itself, it wasn't my fault, but the school institution did not want to pay me to get a Culinary Arts Associate Degree. Like I said, I try everything on me. I don't have anything else. I have no life, so I could just keep going to school to finish my PhD. But I had to drop my classes. I dropped out because it was just a lot, a lot of stuff going on. And I think I needed a full year to a year and a half, possibly two years after my master's degree to pursue it. So, the PhD will be there. It'll be waiting, just like any institution, you know, if one closes, another one opens. But I hope you guys enjoyed this book. Please support me. Please follow me on all social media platforms and also leave comments. Tell me if this book sucked. Tell me if you liked this book. Ask me questions. I have no problems with answering them. Much love and respect and thank-you all for the love and support.

Be blessed!

ABOUT THE AUTHOR

Say hello to Kenneth L. Watson, Jr. a prominent inspirational professional speaker and aspiring best-selling author. His experience and qualifications include the following:

Kenneth L. Watson Jr., an Army Veteran, experienced pieces of his life falling apart due to alcoholism, then decided to fight back. From his life experiences, he has reached a level of calm and serenity where he is rehashing all the demons of past to record in the book *12 Faces of Sober*.

After four years of sobriety, he reaches out to people like himself. Moreover, he speaks through this book to those who suffer post-military life, drug abuse, domestic violence, inequality, mental health, and all sorts of struggles that drive them to alcoholism.

After finding his rooting, he graduated in Strategic Media Communications from St. Cloud State University in 2018.

He continued working on his ideas he collected for the

book over the years.

Within this book, he reaches out to people and reflects the struggles he faced even after sobriety. Kenneth highlights the importance of a support system even in sober days. His struggles, his experiences found in his book, *12 Faces of Sober*, could help many people relate and find solace.

He prides himself in being sober, and why wouldn't he?

He has seen a lot, suffered a lot, known loss, known failure, and surfaced out of it all. It has not been a smooth ride, twelve years in alcoholism, and losing a lot due to it; he comes out as a hero.

He believes that he can give support in this way for many people and wants to build a community of sufferers and survivors to come together to lift each other.

Made in the USA
Columbia, SC
10 September 2020

17902614R00062